ERRANT AFFIRMATIONS

ALSO AVAILABLE FROM BLOOMSBURY

Beckett's Words, David Kleinberg-Levin
Poetry and Revelation, Kevin Hart
The Ethics of Time, John Panteleimon Manoussakis

ERRANT AFFIRMATIONS

On the philosophical meaning of Kierkegaard's religious discourses

DAVID J. KANGAS

BLOOMSBURY ACADEMIC
LONDON • NEW YORK • OXFORD • NEW DELHI • SYDNEY

BLOOMSBURY ACADEMIC
Bloomsbury Publishing Plc
50 Bedford Square, London, WC1B 3DP, UK
1385 Broadway, New York, NY 10018, USA
29 Earlsfort Terrace, Dublin 2, Ireland

BLOOMSBURY, BLOOMSBURY ACADEMIC and the Diana logo
are trademarks of Bloomsbury Publishing Plc

First published 2018
This paperback edition first published in 2022

Copyright © David J. Kangas, 2018

David J. Kangas has asserted his right under the Copyright,
Designs and Patents Act, 1988, to be identified as Author of this work.

For legal purposes the Acknowledgements on p. vii constitute
an extension of this copyright page.

All rights reserved. No part of this publication may be reproduced or
transmitted in any form or by any means, electronic or mechanical,
including photocopying, recording, or any information storage or retrieval
system, without prior permission in writing from the publishers.

Bloomsbury Publishing Plc does not have any control over, or responsibility for,
any third-party websites referred to or in this book. All internet addresses given
in this book were correct at the time of going to press. The author and publisher
regret any inconvenience caused if addresses have changed or sites have
ceased to exist, but can accept no responsibility for any such changes.

A catalogue record for this book is available from the British Library.

A catalogue record for this book is available from the Library of Congress.

ISBN: HB: 978-1-3500-2005-4
PB: 978-1-3503-6636-7
ePDF: 978-1-3500-2004-7
ePub: 978-1-3500-2006-1

Typeset by RefineCatch Limited, Bungay, Suffolk

To find out more about our authors and books visit
www.bloomsbury.com and sign up for our newsletters.

CONTENTS

Acknowledgements vii
A Note on the Texts viii
Preface ix

Introduction   1

PART ONE Inversions of thought and speech: the edifying discourses (1843–1844)   13

1 Affirming time: discourse on the expectancy of faith (1843)   15

2 The gift of being: "Every Good and Perfect Gift Comes Down from Above" (1843)   27

3 Undergoing time: discourses on patience (1843–44)   45

4 Human lack: to need God is a human being's highest perfection (1844)   67

PART TWO Occasions of affirmation: occasional discourses (1845)   79

5 The non-place of truth: discourse on confession (1845)   81

6 On being-together-with-death: discourse "At a Graveside" (1845)   97

PART THREE Bloomings: discourses on "The Lily of the Field and the Bird of the Air (1847, 1849)   113

7   Against care: discourses on the lilies of the field and the birds of the air (1847)   115

8   Lily-bird-being/joy without condition: *The lily of the field and the bird of the air* (1849)   135

Postscript: the edifying and the tragic   169

Notes   173
Index   189

ACKNOWLEDGEMENTS

I wish to acknowledge Alejandro and Daniela and Jason and Meg for their friendship in exigent circumstances. Thanks also to George Pattison and Vanessa Rumble for their support over the years and also to Jeffrey Hanson, editor of this series.

A NOTE ON THE TEXTS

All of the translations in this book are my own. Citations are from the Danish *Søren Kierkegaards Skrifter*, abbreviated as *SKS* and referenced by volume number. I have also supplied reference to the English translation by Howard and Edna Hong with abbreviations as follows:

EUD: *Eighteen Upbuilding Discourses*
TDIO: *Three Discourses on Imagined Occasions*
UDVS: *Upbuilding Discourses in Various Spirits*
WO: *Without Authority*

PREFACE

Kierkegaard, like Nietzsche, was a brilliant polemicist. His polemic against "speculative thought," prosecuted in the pseudonymous writings, grew to all-consuming proportions: he unleashed a scathing critique against the "present age," the media, the established church, against Copenhagen itself. Neighbors turned hostile. His last years saw him on the streets handing out combative pamphlets. The polemical writings are indeed incisive and prescient in their fundamental "No." Yet one cannot help but feel, after long exposure, something of the spirit of resentment animating them. They *calculate* their blows; they demand assent, even obedience; they conjure legions of followers and imitators, simultaneously denouncing and summoning their own herd.

As is known, however, Kierkegaard also wrote religious discourses (*Taler*) alongside the polemical writings. He signed these texts with his own name and financed their publication himself, overseeing every detail of the process: layout, binding, type of paper used, formatting and so on. His first book of discourses (*Two Edifying Discourses*, 1843), published to coincide with *Either/Or*, had a run of five hundred copies. By two years later it had sold two hundred and twenty-two copies; in the years 1844 and 1845 it sold only eleven and nineteen copies, respectively. It was basically the same for all the books of discourses—a wasteful economy, then. And yet it was in reference to these texts that Kierkegaard confided to his journal that he was "overwhelmed with riches," that he "could sit down and write for a day and a night and again for a day and a night, for there was wealth sufficient to it." He produced texts that were by his own reckoning "superfluous," but in the way that a luxury is superfluous. The writing of the discourses was his luxury, his secret indulgence, his excess. To this day, however, these discourses mostly remain, unlike the polemical texts—which one might understand as his *duty* to the age—terra incognita, especially among philosophers.

That is perhaps not surprising, though. In the prefaces to the discourses Kierkegaard repeatedly refers to them as "insignificant," comparing them to a "little flower hidden in a great forest," which "desire only to remain in the hidden, just as they came to be in concealment." So there is perhaps nothing to lament in their lack of reception. It would moreover be entirely misplaced, out of keeping with their spirit and the letter, for a book on the discourses to claim to "fill a gap" in the literature. Even so, for *this* reader, the discourses are the place where Kierkegaard ventures most freely in thought. What resounds is the affirmation that "there is a today, with an infinite emphasis upon *is*." Today—is. To think with sufficient emphasis this conjuncture, this intensification of being, imposes the most rigorous demands on existence: to bloom like the lily, which neither toils nor spins, and to take wing like the bird, which neither reaps nor sows nor stores up in barns.

What follows is not a systematic exposition of the philosophical content of the religious discourses but rather a series of readings that follow a certain trajectory. A systematic exposition of a "philosophy of the edifying discourses," while certainly possible, would be misplaced. The edifying discourse works like the work of art: in giving time and space to the gift of being they dilate the cramped attunement of the human being as informed by care, that is, by the project structure and the all-ravenous effort at knowledge, technique and manipulation. In this very dilation they create room to breathe, the very breath of affirmation. To read an edifying discourse is to find one's way, each time again, to that point from which the dilation spreads. Even if themes repeat, they can never be taken for granted or stabilized in a system; they must be uncovered again in their originality, starting from the horizon opened within the discourse itself.

Introduction

The title of this book risks misunderstanding: what would a philosophical reading of Kierkegaard's religious discourses amount to? Certainly not an effort to separate out some purely philosophical core from these writings, which would imply an artificial split between the philosophical and the religious. A philosophical reading will rather indicate the tracing of a problematic opening *internal* to the discourses themselves. Precisely in their character as "religious"— though Kierkegaard will name them variously "edifying," "occasional," "godly" or "Christian"—the discourses achieve a philosophical radicality, an effort to think beyond the terms of the inheritance bequeathed by Descartes and repeated so profoundly in speculative idealism. It is not only a question of finding a decisive transcendental problematic concerning "the subject" at the heart of these texts—which there is—but of discerning in them a mode of affirmation that is oblique to discourses organized around knowledge. If one wishes an analogue to this problematic—but only that—it may be found in Plotinus' separation of *nous* from *logismos* (of "intellect" or "spirit" from reasoning), or in Spinoza's distinction between intuitive knowledge and discursive knowledge. The religious discourse is *certain* of the urgency of this distinction and knows where to place the emphasis.

Relevant to these distinctions is that, in his prefaces, Kierkegaard formulaically disavows *authority* and, with it, the role of preaching and teaching. What makes this disavowal necessary is much more than, as is sometimes said, Kierkegaard had not been ordained and so was not invested with the ecclesiastical authority to publish *Taler*.[1] The authority disavowed concerns not merely the speaker but also the content spoken about. The discourses do not, namely, elaborate some given, normative content, whether theological or moral; they are not dogmatic texts. Instead, Kierkegaard develops his concepts *starting from* an originary experience with being, an experience inaccessible to because occluded by normalized modes of thought. This work is critical and phenomenological at its core.

Thus, all the discourses aim at an "inversion of thought and speech" in which familiar concepts are overturned in their normalized signification and are invested with a difficult and extraordinary sense. To read the discourses within an ethical or theological register, for example, would be to retreat to the horizon of authority that these discourses disavow. The key to reading the discourses is to find that fulcrum, that point where Kierkegaard gestures to a more originary undergoing of reality, where a certain violence done to ordinary concepts becomes necessary. The discourse says "what ordinary language is not inclined to say." To read a discourse is to follow a concept—such as "faith," "patience" or "confession"—as it is being born, in its repetition; it is to grasp it as it emerges out of an originary sense of what being signifies. Until one discerns why an inversion of thought and speech is necessary, why inherited concepts must necessarily burst, one has not read the discourse.

This is what makes the discourses so demanding. The discourses remain unintelligible, or simply boring, until one discerns the sense of reality both presupposed and articulated in them. They could pass, on a first or even a second reading, for pious sermons. Even Kierkegaard's cousin, upon reading one of his discourses, expressed disappointment that they lacked the wit and verve of his "aesthetic" writings. If one sticks it out for a "third" reading, however, there emerges—like a palimpsest—that which changes everything: the sudden glimpse of an experience of being that cannot be well formulated in normalized concepts or common sense "sayings." Everything must be undone and redone. But this requires patience.

A philosophical reading, excavating the sense of reality presupposed in the discourses just as much as expressed in them, must thus be distinguished in principle from a moral-theological reading. The temptation toward the latter is great, however, since the discourses themselves traverse what seems like intractably moral and theological terrain: not only do they at essential points invoke the theme of obligation, of the "Thou Shalt," but they deal with moral and theological virtues like faith, patience and love. In addition, Kierkegaard inherits and freely deploys his theological heritage, constantly invoking "God" and human existence as "before God." Finally, whatever Kierkegaard may call the discourses—variously "edifying," "occasional," "Christian," "godly,"—all of the discourses have *edification* as their innermost task. Does not edification involve a moral-theological horizon? Before one can perceive the insufficiency of a moral-theological reading a clearer, even though preliminary, concept of the edifying is needed. What is "the edifying?"

In the prefaces to his discourses Kierkegaard makes a clear distinction between "edifying discourses" and "discourses *for* edification." The latter would take edification, the state of being or feeling edified, as the end-goal toward which the discourse is supposed to lead; the discourse would then be a means to that end. Yet in drawing the distinction between edifying discourses and discourses for edification, Kierkegaard disavows this conception of the edifying—along with its conception of writing as writing *for*—because it presupposes that the writer of the discourse is in possession of something the reader is not, namely, knowledge of what edifies and what it is to be edified. It presupposes the authority relation of master and disciple. Kierkegaard, however, could not be clearer: the author of these discourses *is not a moral or theological teacher*. The edifying discourse itself is thus disentangled from any dialectic of recognition, it "goes out like a messenger, but not like a messenger who comes back again."[2] The author relinquishes it from any purposive horizon: the discourse becomes, as Kierkegaard stresses, *superfluous*: "the discourse wishes to be only what it is, a superfluity (*Overflødighed*)."[3]

This must be grasped with its full categorial force: the being of the discourse is to be superfluous. The discourses therefore do not fill any gaps, for example in moral or theological knowledge. They make no contribution to the question "What ought to be done?" That they are superfluous means that they are not *for anything*—not even for edification! They have no intrinsic in-order-to. We are thus presented with an essential distinction: the discourses are edifying according to a quality internal to themselves, without being *for* edification. They are edifying in their very superfluity, their "uselessness." Kierkegaard can compare the discourse to an "insignificant little flower hidden by a great forest, sought neither for its splendor nor its fragrance nor its nutriments."[4]

It would be easy to overlook such a little flower, in other words, to miss the edifying—in particular, by the reader who is seeking a moral or theological program. This is why Kierkegaard reiterates in all his prefaces that the discourse follows an essentially errant path: it goes out wandering, seeking "that singular one" whom he calls "*my* reader." Who is "that singular one?" The one who has been singularized by force of existence itself, exposed to what Kierkegaard calls "the nothing" (*Intetheden*), affected by the superfluity of being. Existence is not "for" anything, anymore than the edifying discourse. But to be exposed to the nothing, affected by the superfluity of being—to have become that singular one—is the condition for reading the edifying discourse. Only that singular one will have ears for its problematic.

What then is edification? The edifying discourse does not instruct; instead, it expands and marks out this prior attunement of the reader to the surplus of being; it elicits it, brings this forward against the dominant reading of surplus as lack. In place of lack, it discovers affirmation. Certainly this involves an "inversion of thought and speech" since the superfluity of being is habitually understood in terms of *lack*. In particular, those traditions deemed "metaphysical," traditions whose purpose it is to set life upon an ultimate ground or vis-à-vis some ultimate end-goal—to demonstrate its moral or theological "why"—cover over the superfluous character of being. A *principle* is set at the origin. Indeed, lack has always carried practical and mesmeric force: lack is not only the condition of the project, but the condition of a desire (*eros*) that orients existence around a transcendent absolute, a first principle or final end-goal. Lack has the magic power of the negative.

The edifying discourse, rejecting lack, brings the surplus of being forward as the *measure of human existence*. To begin to take this as the measure, to take surplus as surplus—Kierkegaard will say "gift"—is already to be edified. It is namely to be *built up* from the origin, remade as it were, starting from the outbreak of something affirmative. Being "built up" in this sense is radically opposed to constituting oneself through projects or upon the basis of a transcendent desire. Taking the surplus of being as the measure of the human is rather a work of essential patience; and, in as much as it exposes one to "the nothing," it is a work of faith. The latter two—patience and faith—can no longer be understood within a moral-theological register as virtues for example, but rather as modes expressive of an unconditioned affirmation of reality.

This is indeed where the discourses really tend: toward an affirmation of reality that is unconditioned, that is, without cause or occasion. Kierkegaard considers such affirmation in the most sustained way in his reflections on the Matthean text concerning the "lily of the field and the birds of the air"—a biblical passage he took up in three separate books.[5] The lily of the field and the bird of the air, which Kierkegaard regards as "teachers" of the essential, are emblems of a joy that is without conditions, a joy "over nothing." The lily and the bird realize in themselves the superfluity of being: they have their being outside projects, outside care; they exist "for nothing," that is, they take the measure of their being, not from a horizon of the project—and thus out of fundamental attunement of care—but from the gratuity of being itself. Such joy indicates an excess of affirmation over any cause or occasion, an affirmation of reality itself, of being in its superfluity. For Kierkegaard this is a human possibility but it necessarily appears, to usual modes of affirmation, as perverse or errant. Hence, the "Thou Shalt:" an imperative is needed, not as a moral principle, but as an intervention, a disruptive factor. Moreover, because such an affirmation is "over nothing," because it in principle excludes the usual ways of affirming—through the project, for example—it is inseparable from the "infinite sorrow." The human being is not endorsed in its own terms, hence the reference to the lily of the field and the bird of the air. The lily and the bird exist simultaneously with infinite sorrow and unconditioned joy. An affirmation of this sort is neither morally nor theologically founded; it is an errant affirmation.

The edifying discourses are threatened by a misunderstanding from another side. Ever since Hegel and even more explicitly in Freud the edifying has been associated with *consolation*. The modern critique of edification presupposes that it is organized around wish-fulfillment: the desire that reality be otherwise than it is. Freud, like Hegel, rejects the need for consolation as infantile: one ought to be able to take reality as it is, without the "sugar coating." Projecting wishes as the horizon of the interpretation of the real, however profound the wishes, is basically immature. For Freud, the striking and devastating fact was that the picture of reality emergent in religious discourses conformed exactly to how one would *wish* reality to be. Thus Freud recalls the "god of Logos," and recovers the inner calling of philosophy as a tragic orientation toward knowledge, toward truth, at whatever cost. Tragic Oedipus, willing knowledge of the truth, of his *own* truth, even though it will destroy him, is the exemplar of the human position.[6]

Are not Kierkegaard's edifying discourses organized around consolation? One must first note that they presuppose something essentially destructive: namely, the critique or dismantling of representational modes of thought that are rooted in the human power of imagination (what Freud calls "wish-fulfillment"). To represent reality is to form a suitable human image of things—that is, an image of things in which the human position, human power, is endorsed. In and for representation reality appears as the setting of the human *project* and the project is taken as grounded in a transcendent desire. One can conceive the entire trajectory of idealism, from Kant to the early Heidegger, from this point of view. In its modern mode, representational thinking takes the power of consciousness to achieve presence to itself, to get a grip on itself, as fundamental. In a word, it takes consciousness as its own origin, as the measure of itself and its "other." Kierkegaard's discourses, on the way to finding an affirmation, relentlessly pursue a critique of representation and, along with this, of the project. Essentially implicated in this critique is what Kierkegaard calls "the wish" (*Ønsket*).

The philosophical meaning of this critique, in particular, is rooted in the fact that Kierkegaard explicitly understands its ontological stakes: it is for him about the *being* of the human being. As the discourses make clear, for Kierkegaard the human project of "self-overcoming" constitutes, as it were, the *Ur*-ideology that has to be demystified. The ultimate ontological counter-structure that he identifies and elaborates in phenomenological terms, as the basis of his destructive critique, is that of the self's being entrapped in itself, riveted to itself, absolutely incapable of an assertion of power vis-à-vis its being and therefore absolutely *in-capable*. Everything idealism thought of as "the subject"—the power to posit itself, to project itself and realize itself and ultimately to create itself[7]—is shown to be derivative upon this more radical structure.[8] The edifying discourses bring thinking back to an origin that cannot be mastered and to an ultimate situation of in-capability that defines human reality. This is why the moral horizon—whether Stoical, Aristotelean, Kantian, or some form of Christianity that incorporates these in its determination of human reality—cannot be ultimate. Until the "subject" explicitly discerns, attends to, and undergoes the ultimate situation of being in-capable, until "the wish" is relinquished, there is no edification.

However, on this condition, the discourses do not despise consolation either: not consolation as rooted in wish-fulfillment, but as being joyful, as affirmation itself.

And what of God in these discourses? The fact that Kierkegaard inherits and freely deploys a theological conceptuality and vocabulary is an occasion for another misunderstanding of these discourses. Contemporary philosophical interest presupposes Heidegger's critique of "onto-theology," that is, the reduction of the problem of being to the problem of *a highest being*. For Heidegger, the onto-theological gesture—the effort to ground all beings on a highest being, a first cause, an ideal instance, an ultimate principle—was constitutive of "metaphysics." The problem with metaphysics: it occludes the more fundamental meaning of being, the event of disclosure, the *coming-to-presence* of things. If metaphysics is dominated by the "principle of reason," that all things exist on the foundation of a reason, a cause, that one can "render an account" of the being of all things through a prior reason—whether founded in "God" or some other absolute—Heidegger opens thinking to the gratuity of things, their groundlessness.[9] The proper task of thinking is not to account for things by reference to an ultimate principle or origin (an *archē*) but rather to account for how this understanding of the philosophical task—namely, metaphysics or onto-theology—itself came to be, how metaphysical thinking emerged as *one* of the possibilities of thinking, and to move to "another beginning" in thought.

From the purview of the critique of ontotheology one cannot invoke God, or parallel concepts, like eternity, without reproducing a discourse whose exhausted possibilities are already being felt and experienced. The task of thinking is precisely to clarify what it means to witness this end. Is affirmation in Kierkegaard's sense predicated upon the existence of a highest being? Are the discourses dedicated to the discovery and elaboration of *reasons* to affirm?

In fact, the logic of the edifying discourse does not go the way of grounding and reasons; in particular, affirmation is incompatible with, and contrary to, the *positing* of a highest being as its condition. The problem is with positing. Any act of positing—and belief is an act that posits some existence—produces, as its essential counter-effect, doubt (*Tvivl*). Belief and doubt are strictly correlated, two sides of the same coin: both maintain a relation of exteriority to the object; both carry within themselves the essential possibility of being "double-minded" and irresolute. A highest being, held within an act of positing, would be the source of an infinite dialectic of belief and doubt—a "bad" infinity in Hegel's sense. The discourses, therefore, though maintaining a pure affirmation—or rather *because* of this affirmation—neither presuppose nor lead to the belief in the existence of a highest being. The whole structure of belief and doubt is rather set aside. It is replaced by the attunement Kierkegaard calls "faith" (*Troen*).

It is true, though, that Kierkegaard's discourses constantly invoke God and think human reality, in its essential determination, as "before God" (*for Gud*). "Before God" means in the face of, exposed to, under the gaze of; it names something inescapable about human existence, that which cannot be evaded. In this regard the discourses speak of an essential choice confronting the human being: between God and world or God and "mammon." This is an inescapable either/or concerning the fundamental character of one's existence. But is the choice, for example between God and world, the choice between a highest, transcendent being and the field of immanent possibilities called "the world?" Not at all. As Kierkegaard makes clear in a number of discourses, God doubles as both the object of choice, what is chosen, and that which conditions the very possibility of the choice. In the latter sense "God" names the condition of the possibility of a choice that concerns the fundamental attunement of the human being. "Before God" means under the inescapable, absolute pressure of a choice concerning the fundamental attunement of one's being. To relate to God, to assume one's existence "before God," to assert that God exists, is inseparable from—indeed identical to—a confrontation with what fundamentally and essentially determines one's own being.

Kierkegaard's discourses thus articulate the relation to God *as* the relation to that in one's self whereby the self is exposed to what it can neither posit nor master—to its own incapability. In the discourse "To Need God is the Human Being's Highest Perfection" (1844) he enunciates the principle: "Insofar as a person does not know himself in such a way that he knows that he himself is capable of nothing at all, he does not actually become conscious in the deeper sense that *God is*."[10] Expressed more concisely: "To know oneself in one's nothingness is the condition for knowing God."[11] To know God is inseparable from grasping the being of the human being, its fundamental ontological constitution, or rather, is inseparable from *actually undergoing* this condition.

Therefore the elaboration of the fundamental constitution of the human being, the clarification of that *whereby* and that *in which* the human is what it is, coincides with what is called "consciousness that God is." This is not to reduce "theology" to "anthropology," in Feuerbach's terms, because the being of the human being is never thought as self-contained. The human being is rather grasped, *ab origine*, starting from the always-prior event in which it is given and given over to itself—given over to itself in such a way that it cannot evade itself. This is what Kierkegaard calls "the gift." The gift is the gift of being. Vis-à-vis the gift the being of the human being is determined as *in-capable*, as absolutely non-coincident with the instant of its upsurge into being, unable to appropriate it as its own. Rather than determining the properties of a highest being or elaborating a set of theological dogma, then, the discourses clarify the being of the human being according to the gift, that is, the fundamental emplacement and originary temporality and spatiality of the human being. The trajectory of this problematic, which Kierkegaard elaborates phenomenologically, is set explicitly against idealism, in which the subject is grasped as its own foundation and origin.[12]

Even though no systematic articulation of the "philosophy of the edifying discourses" is advisable, then, one can nevertheless summarize several recurrent themes.

1 There is the phenomenological critique of the idealist "subject" by way of a radically different understanding of temporality, namely, temporality as something fundamentally undergone and not emergent through the spontaneous resources of self-consciousness.

2   There is the critique of the "project structure," that is, the notion that the subject is to "actualize" or elaborate itself on the foundation of projected end-goals that it represents to itself *beforehand* and toward which it strives. In place of the project Kierkegaard again and again returns to the impossibility of any "self-overcoming," an impossibility that rests upon the ontologically decisive structure of the self's being entrapped in itself. In this context *doing* is not primary; rather, it is a matter of un-doing and un-learning.

3   Finally, these discourses witness to Kierkegaard's ever-renewed effort to find a language of affirming reality without condition—without, however, escaping the condition of finitude and mortality. It becomes a question of blooming, that is, of becoming *finite without restriction*.

In what follows, I have commented on an embarrassingly small number of discourses. The explanation of this is that I have selected just those discourses I deemed suitable for the articulation of the aforementioned philosophical trajectory: no more, no less. The procedure is admittedly biased. Nonetheless I have tried to remain as faithful as possible to Kierkegaard's Danish texts (what a difference from English!) and to the conceptual horizons opening within each discourse. The result, hopefully, illuminates something of the discourses as a whole—even though, I repeat, the vast terrain of the discourses cannot be totalized under any single trajectory, philosophical or otherwise.

PART ONE

INVERSIONS OF THOUGHT AND SPEECH: THE EDIFYING DISCOURSES (1843–1844)

1

Affirming time: discourse on the expectancy of faith (1843)

Two Upbuilding Discourses, Kierkegaard's first book of discourses, was published on May 16, 1843. It is a discourse on faith, but understands faith as a modality of expectancy (*Forventning*). And, Kierkegaard writes, "expectancy and the future are inseparable ideas."[1] Consequently, the discourse is on faith *as* a modality of the relation to the future and, through the future, to temporality as a whole. Faith is an affirmation of the whole of time, or temporality as such. In this there is reconciliation to reality, a capacity to dwell on the present without being confined to the present. However, faith's affirmation must be distinguished above all from the Hegelian form of reconciliation, which travels the road of *anamnesis*: one is reconciled in a retrospective glance, a gathering up of the whole as a meaningful whole. In faith one is not gathered up into a wholeness of meaning, but into an unreserved welcome of the future. These reflections on expectancy inaugurate the predominant meditation in the first series of "edifying" discourses, eighteen in all: the human relation to its own temporality.

New Year's Day

The setting of Kierkegaard's discourse is New Year's Day. According to custom it is a day to exchange greetings and wishes to each other for the upcoming year, but in this discourse Kierkegaard highlights the ontological significance of the day. It signifies the point of emptiness or nullity of any inceptive moment: "A year has past, a new one begun. Nothing has yet happened in it. The past has concluded; the present is not; only the future is, which is not."[2] The moment of inception, when isolated, is inseparable from indetermination and nonbeing. Disjoined from any past, but not yet linked to anything determinately anticipatable, the inceptive moment binds the present to emptiness. "New Year's Day," the occasion of the discourse, thus signifies the position of the human being facing the future *as* what is indeterminately open: the future as bare future, as event without content. Only the future is, which is not. This future—which might be called the "absolute future"—is to be distinguished from the future as something determinately representable. Nothing has yet begun enough to form the ground of a determinate anticipation. On New Year's Day temporality is ordained toward the future as toward "indiscernible possibility."

Initially, this relation to the future fuels what Kierkegaard calls "the wish" (*Ønsket*). People wish one another and themselves well; but the wish also conceals a profound problem as regards the human relation to time. The wish trades on the conflation of the future as representable, as concretely anticipatable, with the future as essentially indeterminate: one discovers "the difficulty of wishing something determinate in relation to the indeterminate and indeterminable."[3] The wish seeks to determine or represent the future; yet every wish is necessarily groundless insofar as the future is indeterminate. Recognizing this groundlessness, people contend themselves, Kierkegaard suggests, with wishes "of a more general nature in the hopes that its greater compass will more readily embrace the manifoldness of the future."[4] The very generality of the wish expresses its emptiness. Moreover, if one ventures a more determinate wish—the wish for some definite good for another or for oneself—this runs up against the essential undecideability of every wish: the future, harboring within itself everything that *will have been*, possesses a retroactively transformative power to decide upon what is really good. The concrete good that one wishes someone may show itself, in retrospect, to have been the very thing to bring about their destruction. The future harbors the power to upend and reverse all relations. What to wish for then? Here one falls into perplexity, being overcome by a certain "madness." That which bears upon the meaning that a human life will have had, what intimately shapes it, eludes any mastery or anticipation.

On New Year's Day this essential exposure to time as unmasterable, as what is both essentially indeterminate and imminent, becomes apparent. Thus New Year's Day becomes the moment in time in which explicitly to reflect upon one's relation to time. Faith names a relation to time to be distinguished from the wish. In faith nothing determinate or concretely representable is expected; faith is a relation to the future as the absolute future.

The structure of expectancy

Faith, which is a mode of expectancy toward the future, cannot be clarified without clarifying the structure of expectancy and, as a condition for that, the structure of temporality as such. Kierkegaard's discourse here elaborates in an existential key the implications of the Kantian problematic of time as the "form of inner sense" and anticipates both the Husserlian and Heideggerian analyses of time consciousness.[5]

Consciousness of time signifies a consciousness of the whole of time—not simply of the "present moment," but of the co-givenness of future, present and past. Such time consciousness describes the ontological specificity of the human being: whereas the animal lives "in service to the moment," the human being is originally and ecstatically open[6] to all three temporal dimensions, which mutually implicate one another. However, according to Kierkegaard's analysis, the future obtains a priority over the present and the past insofar as it constitutes the condition, or ground, of the latter: "if there were no future, there would be no past either, and if there were neither future nor past, then a human being would be in bondage like an animal ... his soul captive to the service of the moment."[7] At stake here is a transcendental problematic involving the very genesis and possibility of time consciousness in its full scope.

But according to what logic is the future prioritized in this way? How is it that the relation to the future could constitute the condition for a relation either to the past or to the present? Why is the consciousness of the future the primordial relation to time? The logic here is that of the relation between part and whole: "the future is not a particular, but the whole" (*det Tilkommende er ikke et Enkelt, men det Hele*);[8] or again: "the future is indeed everything, the present a part thereof."[9] Just as the gestalt of a face, for example, offers the whole, the context, in which the nose, the eyes and the mouth first become perceptible in their mutual arrangement as what they are, so too the future offers the context by which the present can be present and the past can be past. The future is prior to the phases of time as the whole is prior to the parts.

Kierkegaard's point is that, in terms of the concretely available modalities of time consciousness—the past, the present and the future—only the future can adequately stand for, or give name to, the context-setting factor through which one can grasp or relate to the part *as* the part. The future is unrestricted, or whole, in that its essential indetermination makes it part of *no already available context*. Even if it is true that the past has an inexhaustible depth, this is an inexhaustibility predicated upon something particular already posited. The indetermination of the past is a relative one.[10] The future is, however, absolute, that is, relative to nothing. The relation to the future is real and intimate, in fact defining the very meaning of interiority, but the future essentially cannot be appropriated. Concretely this means, not only that the future cannot be made determinate, but that the future harbors what the present and the past *will have meant*. The meaning of what one is in the midst of is, therefore, essentially partial. Total meaning is in principle unavailable within the present. Yet it is only on foundation of the relation to the future as the whole that the past and present gain their grounding as parts or phases. The expectancy by which consciousness stands open to the whole thus enables the experience of presence in its partial character, as phases. One could say that the experience of the past and the present are essentially horizonal and the future, precisely as whole, constitutes this horizon at every point.

An essential distinction, bearing centrally upon the problematic of faith, must however be underscored. The absoluteness of the future, the manner in which it constitutes a whole, is normally occluded inasmuch as a *representation* of the future is commonly substituted for the absolute future; the absolute future is thereby reduced to something particular. The future as represented, as concretely anticipatable from a determinate present, is but a *phase* or part of temporality and not "the whole." The relation to the absolute future thus remains in principle distinct from the relation to the represented future—as distinct as from its relation to past and present. Past, present and future, conceived as mutually intertwined and concrete phases of time, all find the condition of their possibility in a relation to the absolute future. The latter is the genuinely transcendental factor, the space within which each temporal phase finds its context. In the strict sense, therefore, the absolute future is not "in" the future, that is, not in the future as projected upon the basis of the present.

Existentially, the difference between the determinate future of representation and the absolute future is legible in the circumstance that the tomorrow we anticipate is never the tomorrow that arrives. There is always a surplus, a surprise or sudden factor, that is the very insignia of the future's wholeness (its open character). The struggle with this surplus defines the most intractable struggle of the human being and defines the context of faith as expectancy.

The struggle with time

For Kierkegaard, having a relation to the future is definitive of the ontological specificity of the human being: "the ability to be occupied with the future is ... a sign of the nobility of human beings; the struggle with the future is the most ennobling."[11] Unlike the animal, the human is not captive to, simply immersed in, the present. The human comes to exist only on condition of a rupture or de-adherence from the present, a standing outside the present while remaining within it. Consciousness of the (absolute) future is the originary mode of standing outside the present, the original "ecstasis," and thereby the ground of time consciousness generally. The future, however, is nothing. The character of this nothing and the human relation to it requires clarification.

Kierkegaard writes: "The future is not; it borrows its power from him himself, and when it has tricked him out of that it presents itself externally as the enemy he has to encounter."[12] This is to construct a little mythos, as it were, to account for the genesis of the future, and thus consciousness of time in general, involving a kind of trick or paralogism: the future, though arising through a power that is the self's own, presents itself to the self as an "outside," something the self stands over against. The future has no being of its own; it *is not*. Standing over against it is standing over against the nothing. Yet the nothing somehow *is*. Whence comes its being? What power is it that the future borrows from the human being on the basis of which it achieves being? It is the human being's power to project itself ahead of itself, or to represent itself *as* something in the open horizon of the future.

This originary projection, however, undergoes a strange lapse: the future, though apparently opening through the self's own projection of itself, somehow presents itself as "outside." Somehow the self, initially the origin of the future, finds itself facing an alien power. That the self's own power could appear to itself in the mode of an outside, in an alienated form, suggests however that this power is not fully under the self's command—in other words, that it is not fully "inside." So there is not only an insidedness to the outside, but an outsidedness to the inside. The self tries to arm itself against the future by transforming it to something determinate and present: "we would try to transform [the future] into something present, something particular, yet the future is not a particular, but the whole."[13] This rift between the future as something represented and the future as "the whole" that escapes all representation is a transcendental one, involved in the very possibility of a self. It suggests that the future is, on the one hand, what is most intimate, yet precisely thereby, in its indetermination, the most threatening.

This ambiguity constitutes the terms of an essential struggle: to struggle with the future becomes the self's struggle with its own self, its own indetermination. Where the self encounters something definite, where there is a clean break between inside and outside, it can employ its full power against the alien object. It retains its identity and continuity. But in relation to the future as the whole, the open, nothing is granted against which power can be deployed. The future in this sense offers no side by which to grip it. Though it bears down as an "enemy" in relation to the self's anticipative and representational powers, it cannot be confronted. Owing to its relation to the future—which indeed constitutes its being—the self can no more master itself, that is, appropriate itself, than it can master the future: "When a person struggles with the future, he learns that however strong he is otherwise, there is one enemy that is stronger—himself; there is one enemy he cannot conquer by himself, and that is himself."[14]

This relation to the future announces what will be a fundamental motif of the edifying discourses: the absolute *incapacity for the human being to achieve a self-overcoming*. A self is bonded to the future as to its own essential indeterminacy. Vis-à-vis itself the human being is exposed to an essential powerlessness: a powerlessness to get a grip on itself, to posit itself, to will itself. This incapacity is identical to its temporality. And yet the struggle with itself— that is, with the future—is the "most ennobling" struggle. The human being receives its ontological distinctiveness in something apparently negative: its powerlessness vis-à-vis itself. This powerlessness is not something static, but ceaselessly imposes itself anew as the very tension of a self. At the very heart of the self's being a scission opens up, therefore, between all forms of power, of project and technique, and the self's "nobility." Faith is born in the context of this essential struggle.

Time under the aspect of victory

If the self cannot master itself or the future through any technique, that is, through any definite application of its power, the discourse still insists that it is possible to "conquer" (*beseire*) the future: faith is a relation to time under the aspect of "victory" (*Seier*). But how is this possible, inasmuch as, in relation to the future, the self undergoes its own absolute incapacity? How is victory possible when any self-overcoming is impossible? To conquer or totalize time is precisely what the self cannot do.

The discourse carefully elaborates faith's relation to time: it is neither resignation, which expects nothing, nor the expectation of any *particular* thing, what Kierkegaard calls "the wish." He writes: "not only the person who expects absolutely nothing does not have faith, but also the person who expects something particular or founds his expectancy on something particular [does not have faith]."[15] The wish relates to the future under the form of a definite representation: it expects this or that; it hopes. Yet the wish, Kierkegaard says, is simply a modality of deception (*Skuffelse*) because it occludes the essential difference between the future as represented and the absolute future. The wish creates a pseudo-continuity between the self and its own future. Resignation, by contrast, involves the effort to starve out any possible disappointment by depriving it of its nourishment in expectation. Resignation is a fundamentally defensive strategy towards time.

Faith, by contrast, expects "victory"—not this or that victory, but victory as such: "you speak of many victories, but faith expects just one—or, more exactly, it expects victory."[16] To expect victory is not the same as to exist in projection ahead of oneself in the representation of future victory. Faith's expectation is not a representation. It is rather a relation to time as such and as a whole. The whole of time cannot be represented or even anticipated in any definite way. Faith is an affirmation of the whole of time prior to and as the condition of the affirmation of the part: faith "is finished (*færdig*) with the future before [it] begins with the present."[17] To be finished with the future is the opposite of projecting oneself ahead of oneself; it is a cutting away from projection so as to abandon oneself to the present. Thus faith immediately expresses itself as a relation to the present: it exists "wholly and indivisibly in the present" (*heel og udeelt i det Nærværende*).[18] Faith does not affirm victory as some definite event. Rather, it carries victory—its affirmation of time as such—*into* each present. The victory of faith, in other words, lies in the act of faith itself: "my expectation [of victory] *is* victory."[19] Faith is in this sense a modality, not of representation, but of *action*. Faith exists, Kierkegaard says, "only in constantly being acquired and [it] is acquired only by constantly being brought forth."[20] Faith is a way of taking up time, of inhabiting time, a task that demands constant renewal. Victory does not inhere in being itself, only in the act—something always to be taken up anew—in which affirmation is achieved. Victory is in the abandonment to the present; it *is* the abandonment to the present.

Faith is therefore an act that grasps time as such, *that there is time*, as already "victory." For what is the measure of time? How is one to decide what time as such and as a whole signifies? The fact that one is always already "within" time precludes any decision on time's meaning founded in knowledge. It is essentially impossible to *know* what time means. Equally impossible, owing to the very nature of the self's inherence in time, is to achieve a self-overcoming: that is, for the self to constitute itself, through the project, as the source and guarantor of the meaning of time. That faith is not in something affirmable but is itself the affirmation means that no temporal event can either confirm or refute it. Yet in relation to this Kierkegaard airs an objection: "An expectancy without a specified time and place is nothing but a deception; in that way one may always go on waiting; such an expectancy is a circle into which the soul is bewitched and from which it cannot escape."[21] If faith's affirmation can neither be confirmed nor refuted by any event, is it not a purely circular posit? In grasping time as a whole under the aspect of victory, doesn't faith execute the metaphysical move *par excellence*: asserting a first principle that, precisely as first, can neither be confirmed nor refuted? Yet with faith it is not a first principle that is asserted; it is a relation to the originary, that is, to time as such—something the soul is always already involved in. The circle thus involves a relation of the soul to its own being: "Certainly in the expectancy of faith the soul is prevented from, so to speak, falling outside of itself into multiplicity; it remains within itself."[22] The soul's remaining in itself is its remaining in complete abandonment to the present. To slip out of this abandonment would be the "greatest evil" that could befall a person because they would then be thrust into a frantic dialectic of hope and doubt, falling outside themselves into the multiplicity of time phases. Faith is saved in its complete abandonment to the present.

However, faith's abandonment to the present is not its simple immersion in the "now." Faith has its condition in a relation to what Kierkegaard calls the eternal: "By the eternal, one can conquer the future, because the eternal is the ground (*Grund*) of the future, and therefore through it the future can be fathomed (*udgrunder*)."[23] The eternal, precisely as ground of the future, is not the abrogation of time but what safeguards the futurity of the future. The eternal holds open the future as future—as fundamentally indeterminate—and this indetermination is therefore already a trace of the eternal. Faith, which expects victory, is no mere recognition of this temporal structure; rather, it grasps it as *what is to be affirmed*. It affirms what cannot appear within the horizon of time: the absolute future. In the strictest sense no temporal event—past, present or future—can become the object of affirmation. Only the eternal as the surplus of the future can be affirmed because affirmation is inherently a movement of excess. The excessive quality of affirmation is exactly what allows it to be carried into the present. Faith surpasses immersion in the present because it is a modality of *beginning with the present*. On the strength of its affirmation it grasps the present "before" the present has begun to be, at its very incipience, and thus it carries affirmation with it into every present.

Conclusion: the logic of faith

Faith is the affirmation of the whole of time. If it preserves a future orientation this is because the whole of time has its phenomenological inscription only as the "other side" of the future, that is, the future in excess to any anticipation or representation. The self is absolutely incapable of determining the absolute future either through knowledge or through its own projects. And yet the self *is* its absolute future. Thus a zone of interiority is exposed in the self's relation to itself—and to time—defined by the impossibility of self-overcoming. Faith is not a weak modality of knowledge (not belief). Its sole context lies rather in its incapacity in its relation to its own being: it finds there something to affirm beyond the affirmation of this or that. Faith's expectation of victory is its affirmation of its own temporal being-as-such; it grasps the outbreak of time as already victory. As opposed to what? It is certainly possible to take time according to a logos of death and catastrophe. According to such a logos, it would be better not to have been born. Once having been born, there is rigor only in measuring oneself against the event of death. This nostalgia for non-being describes the innermost tendency of the tragic interpretation of being. Faith in Kierkegaard's sense is not only a refusal of the tragic, but its actual uprooting. The incipience of time itself, the birth of time into being, is already victory. It will be evident, however, that in principle nothing could guarantee faith's affirmation. It remains essentially a risk, an expectation.

2

The gift of being: "Every Good and Perfect Gift Comes Down from Above" (1843)

In his *Four Upbuilding Discourses* (1843) Kierkegaard devoted two discourses to a textual fragment from James 1:17, a fragment that he would come to call, at the end of his life, his first and only love: "every good gift and every perfect gift is from above" (James 1:17).[1] In taking up this textual fragment, however, Kierkegaard's discourse positions itself with respect to a history of citation, in particular one deriving from the sermons of Meister Eckhart. Eckhart had taken up the same textual fragment several times under the Latin title *Omne datum optimum et omne donem perfectum desursum est*.[2] The Eckhartian provenance of this citation and this discourse will prove crucial to its interpretation if only because Eckhart, more than anyone else, made the figure of the gift resonate with philosophical meaning: the gift is the gift *of being*.

It must be emphasized, however, that Kierkegaard's discourse on the gift does not aim (any more than Eckhart's) at the clarification of a cause or ground of all things. It does not, therefore, aim at that from which rational insight could derive, out of some first principle, an account concerning the genesis of things. Rather, the discourses ask concerning the "hidden place" (*Gjemmested*) or the "source" (*Udspring*)³ of all. For reasons essential to the problematic this origin does not admit of being known. This will have nothing to do with its obscurity or, even less, its remoteness; nor is any "negative theology" at stake here.⁴ Rather, the conditions in which knowledge (or non-knowledge) transpires turn out to be disparate from those in which the gift transpires. Traversing the discourse is a rift between a thinking dominated by categorial intuitions and hence aiming at the production of determinate knowledge and a more radical orientation toward the event whereby there is the given. The gift is affirmed, not in knowledge, but in the incipience of a new orientation itself, a "new beginning."

Ultimately, as befits an edifying discourse, an essentially practical question is at stake in these discourses: what would it mean for the human being to take itself, prior to and apart from all effort, as situated within an order of generosity? Even more, what tasks, what destructions or reversals, would be presupposed in taking *lack itself* according to an order of generosity?

Doubt and the effort at knowledge

Kierkegaard's discourse on the gift begins by recalling the mythical condition of pre-fallen humanity. The philosophical expression of this mythos is realized in the concept of "immediacy," which indicates the condition of the human being prior to the ontologically decisive event of "separation" (*Adskillelsen*) in which there opens a rift between being and appearing: in immediacy, "everything *was* what it *seemed to be*." Prior to the separation of being and appearing any *question* concerning being is in principle impossible: "Adam would not have had time to ask where [everything] came from because everything offered itself in the moment."⁵ Immediacy thus signifies the condition that precedes the event that, in the strict sense, will open philosophy as a discourse of the question: the event of the splitting between *what is* and what *appears to be*. Prior to that event—which coincides with the emergence of phenomena as phenomena—there is no possibility of formulating a question and, as a consequence, no possibility of projecting forth a horizon of knowledge. Moreover, Kierkegaard explicitly links the event of separation to the irruption of time consciousness. Immediacy is perfect adherence to the moment, outside of any temporal projection. It is a condition of plenary presence or pure givenness. In immediacy there is no gift precisely because *all* is gift.

If Kierkegaard recalls the Genesis myth, it is because immediacy and its abrogation is never something simply finished and done with but continues to permeate human existence as a structural moment, albeit in a recessed or "sublated" way. In the recognizably Hegelian way Kierkegaard formulates it, immediacy and its abrogation constitutes a moment that "continually repeats itself in every generation and in every individual."[6] Otherwise put: to the philosopher's eyes the Genesis myth involves a transcendental problematic concerning the originary separation of what is from what appears to be, a problematic that involves the birth of time consciousness. One could say at stake is an originary differing and deferral (to gesture to Derrida's concept of *différance*).[7] In Kierkegaard's language, the moment of separation signifies the emergence of doubt (*Tvivlen*) as a fundamental ontological power. Doubt thus signifies, in this transcendental context, neither a psychological state nor even a methodological commitment (as in Descartes). Rather, it refers back to the originary event of doubling or splitting into two of reality.[8]

Moreover, outside of this doubling of the real, reality could not in principle come into question and thus the effort at knowledge could find no basis. The consequence: far from being able to overcome doubt, knowledge continually reproduces doubt as the condition of its possibility. Knowledge thus remains the essential, mythical temptation of the human being. In the context of a consideration of the gift, however, the question of knowledge is oriented around a particular axis: "what is the good, where is the perfect to be found, out of what origin is it, if it exists?"⁹ Can knowledge (*Kundskaben*) or cognition (*Viden*) produce an intuitively clear concept to make manifest *what* the good is and thus make it available for appropriation? Or are human beings confined to a mere semblance of the good? Can the human being find a measure for itself within the general condition of doubt—that is, within the horizon of appearing being? Can a ground be secured?

However, these questions undergo a certain complication as soon as it is a question of the origin of the good. The one who asks the question seeks not only *what* the good is, but also asks concerning its provenance, namely *wherefrom* it is: "Would he find out what the good and perfect is without knowing where it came from, would he be able to recognize the eternal source without knowing what the good and perfect is?"¹⁰ There is a circle here: what the good is can only be expressed through its provenance; but its provenance can be brought to light only in terms of what it is. To ask concerning the provenance of the good is to seek its original source, which is to say that whereby it is effective; to ask concerning the whatness of the good is to seek a conceptual determination, a norm or criterion, by which it can be recognized. Can knowledge achieve this?

The question has already been answered: doubt is essentially "the stronger" (*den Stærkere*) because every act of knowledge finds its conditioning possibility in doubt. Consequently, the course of knowledge, the effort to determine *what is*, takes shape as an unending proliferation of determinations: "the effectivity of the fruits of knowledge cannot be stopped."¹¹ Amidst the proliferation of knowledge, which proceeds limitlessly, doubt "cunningly" provokes the knower to imagine that he can himself constitute, in a moment of self-gathering, something like a ground or point of orientation. Doubt provokes the thought that "a person can overcome himself through himself" (*ved sig selv kan overvinde sig selv*). One could say this is the siren song of knowledge. Though Kierkegaard does not explicitly identify his reference, the allusion is to Descartes's attempt to establish a *fundamentum inconcussum*, an unshakeable point of self-certainty within the pure presence to itself of consciousness. A cognitive act rendering an intuitively clear concept of the good would here be inseparable from the act by which the subject could produce the good out of the inner spontaneity of its own consciousness. Yet the point of identity that could ground such intuitive knowledge has for Kierkegaard already been abrogated by doubt: the splitting or difference of the real would amount to an insuperable gap in presence between the subject and itself. Doubt is again not reducible to a method; it is rather the ontological event whereby the horizon of knowledge opens. Knowledge cannot place itself beyond the conditions of its possibility and hence a self-overcoming is in principle impossible.

Thus the gift, the effective presence of the origin, cannot be secured through knowledge. Kierkegaard reaffirms this point through the elaboration of a series of aporias relating to the phenomena of gift giving.

The phenomenology of the gift and its destruction

Kierkegaard's discourse is addressed to one in a condition of concern (*Bekymring*) about realizing a relation to the good, not merely as an object of knowledge, but to the good in its effective presence, out of its source. The horizon of knowledge offers no way to the good, which is "from above." The question thus returns: where to find orientation toward the good? A new departure suggests itself from the biblical text: "If you, who are evil, know how to give good gifts to your children, how much more will your heavenly Father give good things to those who ask him?" (Mt.7:11). This scriptural text embeds within itself an image (*et Billede*) of the most immediate affirmation: what could be more readily affirmed than the image of a parent giving good gifts to children? To what extent, the question now is, can this *image* of the gift provide orientation in the movement of achieving an effective relation to the good?

If the scriptural text is able to offer orientation, we shall see, it will only be on condition of a destruction of its status as an image. It will be necessary to "forget the imaginal in favor of the actual" (*glemmer det Billedlige over det Virkelige*). The discourse thus takes a destructive turn: the immediately affirmable phenomena of giving and receiving gifts, Kierkegaard shows, is exposed to a set of aporias that place the reality of giving and of the gift in doubt.[12] Kierkegaard shows, *in principle*, that something imaginary must always belong to the concrete actions of giving and receiving gifts—so much so that it becomes necessary to see that, in reality, "nothing good and perfect exists in the world." When a father gives a gift to a son and the son receives a gift, the gift itself, what is given and received, does not surpass the ontological status of an image. But why not? Implicated in giving, as a structural and therefore non-effaceable moment, is an essential gap between knowing *what it means* to give and actually being *able* to give: "Consequently, a human being can know [what it means] to give good gifts, but he can't know whether he is giving a good gift; likewise, the evil person can know [what it means] to give an evil gift, but he can't know whether he is giving an evil gift."[13]

The conditions of gift giving include within themselves a blind spot: namely, the *incalculability* of the effect of giving upon the one receiving. On the side of the giver, there is no way to guarantee or foresee the good efficacy of the gift, no way to secure the good intention that motivates the gift. Even the most salutary intention, even the most recognized good that could be given, cannot be counted upon to bring about what it intends. The safest gift can be the most dangerous, the most trivial, the most consequential. Similarly, the intention to do evil cannot escape this moment of incalculability: a wound may redound to the benefit of the wounded. Between the intention to give, in other words, and the actual giving (and receiving), there is an essential discordance that cannot be smoothed over. The assertion that a gift has really been given, therefore, can only be sustained by appeal to an imaginary continuity, a perfectly calculable effect.

Apart from this incalculable moment, Kierkegaard elaborates another blind spot affecting the possibility of gift giving. Certain gifts might be possible to know and grasp as in and for themselves good—consequently, as good apart from their effects. Or are there no intrinsic goods the giving of which must also, therefore, itself be good? What about the good of friendship, for example? Or, to return to the example in the biblical text Kierkegaard cites, the gift of a father's love for his son? Do not such acts realize what it means to give? But here too, even in this intimacy of giving, there is a blind spot: a human being "can know what the good is as something in and for itself perfect, but whether he gives it, he cannot know."[14] There could be certainty about the gift, certainty about the intention to give, but whether one *actually* gives what one intends to give necessarily escapes the giving. At what point, for example, can a friend authenticate the giving of friendship? Granted, Kierkegaard says, by the usual "indifferent" reckoning, perhaps there is no problem. Gift giving generally goes smoothly, but only because its aporias are masked by an imaginary continuity. Yet in a condition of concern, where something is really at stake in giving or not giving, when the effects of giving (or not) are consequential, it must remain in suspension *whether* the gift has been given.

In a complicated passage Kierkegaard elaborates the general conditions motivating the destruction of the gift-image: "So nothing good and perfect exists in the world. For the good either exists in such a way that by the very fact of coming into existence it becomes a doubtful good—but a doubtful good is no good, and a good that could only be in such a way that it cannot come into existence is not the good—or it exists in such a way that it is conditioned by a presupposition which must exist but which is not itself the good."[15] What earlier was identified as a blind spot for knowledge—the gap of incalculability—is here identified as the movement of coming into existence itself, that is, the very movement of realization. A certain aporia arises here: on the one hand, the movement of coming into existence coincides with a *becoming indeterminate* of the good—and this, not as a matter of chance, but essentially; on the other hand, if the good is grasped under some determination, such determination could only reside in a condition lying exterior to the good itself—for example, the good would be definably good in reference to some finite lack it fulfills, in which case it would be relativized. Also explicitly rejected in the above passage is any notion of the good as an ideal form immune to becoming. The good can in no sense be regarded as a transcendent or transcendental ideal, that is, an eidetic object pole of striving; rather, the good is good only in its effective realization, the movement of its becoming.[16] The discourse, however, has made that becoming problematic. Hence, Kierkegaard returns to the question again: can the gift be clarified in the path of its realization; where and how is it effective?

Within the horizon of doubt and knowledge—which is to say within the horizon of what appears and thus becomes subject to a possible cognition—the gift loses its content. Either, through knowledge, it is reduced to something given, some objective determination that the knower represents to himself; or through an intention-to-give it runs aground on the incalculable nature of reality itself. If the gift is to be sustained, therefore, it must be thought from a different side. From where? Kierkegaard returns to the biblical text to retrieve a concept: the good and perfect gift must be thought rigorously as what "comes from above" (*kommer herovenfra*): "what is the good? It is that which is from above. What is the perfect? It is what is from above. From where does it come? From above." The whole discourse now turns on the sense of this phrase "from above." To think the gift out of its provenance from above will be to think in relation to its original source and effectiveness—and consequently, to think it, no longer as an image, but in its actuality and truth.

Kierkegaard gives an essential indication of how to begin to understand the direction of the gift in the following: "the way to the good, to the hiding place of the good, [no one] knows, for there is no way there (*ingen Vei derhen*), but all good and all perfect gifts come *down* from above." Here the directionality of the gift—from above—is directly opposed to a movement of methodical development. Kierkegaard's reference here—left unstated but perfectly clear in relation to the previous development of doubt—is to the whole development of a founded knowledge, from Descartes to Fichte. Within this "modern metaphysics of the subject" the milieu of self-consciousness, the subject's power to remain present to itself, or re-present itself, was incorporated as a foundation *from which* progressively to pursue knowledge. The true and actual could only present itself to and within this foundation, in the clarity of evidence. Within this configuration, self-consciousness, as presence to itself, constitutes the ultimate condition in which anything can be received, taken up, known. What cannot manifest itself in the milieu of self-certain consciousness can claim no actuality or truth.

That the good comes not only "from above," but from a place inaccessible to the reach of method thus signifies, in the first place, that the condition through which the gift is received does *not* lie on the side of self-consciousness. Self-consciousness itself does not possess, either contingently or transcendentally, the capacity to receive the gift. In light of the whole previous development concerning doubt and knowledge, one can see why not: if the condition for receiving the gift somehow already preceded the gift—even though transcendentally—this would open a rift between the gift and its possible reception. In terms of a transcendental structure like this, the gift could be thought as essentially *possible*, but not in its "truth and actuality." Kierkegaard's discourse seeks the articulation of the condition of the actual realization of the gift.

The whole previous development of the discourse has cast in doubt—not whether there is the authentic intention to give, nor whether giving gifts concretely takes place, for example between a father and a son—but whether the gift can be *thought* as something actual and true. Or is the gift merely an image that dissipates upon contact with reality? The biblical text already contained a rider to put the reader on notice: "If you, being evil. . . ." In effect the biblical text had already heralded its own destruction insofar as it remained a discourse organized around an image. The question now is whether, for thought, the discourse on the gift can be sustained. Or, to put it more precisely in Kierkegaard's terms, the question now is not *whether* the discourse on the gift can be sustained, but what are the conditions—both conceptually and existentially—in which it *actually is*? For that there is a gift, that the gift is real and actual, can at no moment be put into a conditional: *if* there is the gift.[17] As shall be seen, this is not owing to the self-certifying nature of the gift, but to a displacement of conditions in the gift event.

The biblical text, then, initially set forth as a guide capable of orienting the human being around the gift as something affirmable, shows itself, upon reflection, only to promote a "melancholy recollection … of life's first unforgettable impression." In this way the biblical text still wholly conforms to what Kierkegaard calls an "imagistic discourse," a discourse incapable of sustaining the actual expression of the good and therefore in need of being thought otherwise.

The (un)condition of the gift

Kierkegaard's discourse now takes up its essential development: what is the inner structure of the gift event? The question is now, in Kierkegaard's language, to find the actual and true expression of the gift, to think through a concept of the gift in explicit difference from its image. What in general renders the gift doubtful, or what makes the gift in general dependent upon some imaginary continuity, is that the conditions for receiving the gift lie external to the giving of the gift—as indeed to the gift itself. The actual and true gift, therefore, must presuppose no other condition than itself—it must signify a giving that is wholly without conditions, or unconditional. In particular, this would mean a gift that is: 1) not aimed at filling some already existing lack; 2) not made possible on the ground of some prior (transcendental) structure of receptivity on the part of the recipient; 3) not motivated, on the part of the giver, by any particular intention to give—or, more generally stated, not be mediated by any representation. The gift must, in every way, presuppose itself or constitute its own condition: which is to say, contain within itself both *the conditions of itself and the conditions of its reception*. In several dense passages Kierkegaard formulates this unconditioned structure:

> For God is the only one who gives in such a way that he gives the condition along with—the only one who, in giving, has already given . . . This condition [which makes it possible to receive the gift], God has himself given, for otherwise the good would not be a gift; this condition is, again, itself a perfection, for otherwise it would not be a perfect gift . . . *The condition is a gift of God and a perfection that makes it possible to receive the good and perfect gift.*

These texts all speak to the condition (*Betingelsen*) of the gift in an absolute sense: not only to the condition of the reception of the gift but also to the condition of the giving of the gift. The condition of the gift is in every case the same: the gift presupposes itself, that is, realizes itself along with the conditions of its own receptivity—this is what makes it an unconditioned movement. Consequently, the good and perfect gift must already be realized in a giving which makes it possible to receive the good and perfect gift. The gift must always already be received, and given, prior to being received and given. The gift lies prior to its own givenness. This is why Kierkegaard explicitly emphasizes that God is the only one who, in giving, has *already* given. It is also why, in all strictness, the gift comes "from above:" from above signifies that the gift arrives always prior to itself, which is to say, always prior to its being known, received, recognized, determined. Through the gift human reality is thus subjected to a unique temporality: it is thoroughly determined by an always-prior instant in which it was enabled to receive itself. The gift makes the self precede itself in being. The gift coincides here with a receptivity—not, however, in the manner of a receptive power that would fall, transcendentally, on the side of an already existing subject, but a receptive power that would constitute the very subjectivity of the subject. The possibility of receiving the gift is already the gift. According to the gift, therefore, all forms of capability have their source, not in the inner resources of self-consciousness, but in an original incapability.

Eckhartian provenance: God as gift

It is at this point worth pausing to consider the provenance of Kierkegaard's reflections on the gift. Through whatever historical mediations it came to be, Kierkegaard's discourse repeats the essentials of Meister Eckhart's thinking of the gift.[18] What is particularly important to emphasize here, however, is how the concept of God undergoes necessary reformulation in terms of the event of the gift. In a sentence that has an almost direct parallel in Eckhart, Kierkegaard writes: "What is the good? It is that which is from above. What is the perfect? It is that which is from above. From where does it come? From above. *What is the good? It is God. Who is it that gives it? It is God* …"[19] Such sentences are easily overlooked, but they must be accorded their fundamental significance in the interpretation of the discourse. In terms of this passage God is both the giver and what is given. In terms of the structure of the gift already articulated, this *must* be the case: if God were not both giver and given, if the gift were something other than God, or God were something other than the gift, this would insert an external condition into the giving of gift and reduce the gift to an object given. The gift event would no longer constitute its own condition.

Where God is thought both as giver and given, however, what does this say? It says God "is" the giving-of-God and the giving-of-God "is" God. God is both wholly giver and wholly given—but this identity transpires only in, or as, the giving itself. Thus, *in the gift event itself*, there is no difference between giver, given and gift. There is, in all strictness, no space for thinking God as a "highest being" who would somehow maintain a separate existence from the giving itself. Like Eckhart, Kierkegaard is here thinking God according to a *verbal* formula rather than a nominal one: not *a* being, God "is" the giving by which there are beings. Even more precisely: God is the giving by which beings are enabled to receive being. Although, it is true, Kierkegaard himself does not emphasize the point or make it the explicit object of analysis—*unlike* Eckhart in that sense—all of the conceptual structures already articulated in relation to the gift presuppose this revaluation in the concept of God. To relate to God *is* to relate to an event of giving that, in terms of its structure, has always already taken place.

The great overturning

In the effort to think its actual and true expression Kierkegaard's discourse has shown the fantasmatic status of what are normally called gifts. Only when the gift is thought as the gift of being—as the event in which being is granted, occurring prior to anything that could condition it—is the gift-image surpassed by its true expression. Only the gift of being is the gift "in and for itself," the good and perfect gift. The edifying discourse now takes on the task of clarifying human existence according to the gift, starting from the unconditioned event of the gift. At issue is a "new beginning" in which the "old order of things"—the order in which the effort at knowledge reigns supreme—is overturned and human existence is gripped by an essential need (*Trang*) not addressed or fulfilled by the work of knowledge. According to the logic already elaborated, this need for the gift is already the gift insofar as the gift brings about the conditions of its own reception. Thus to think human existence according to the gift it is necessary to think it organized around a need that is not in any way a lack— indeed, it is to think human existence *outside of all lack*. Such a conception, however, necessarily implies a "great overturning" (*stor Omvæltning*)[20] in normalized modes of thought.

Kierkegaard makes the difference between need and lack an explicit problematic:"Earthly need [i.e. lack] is no perfection, but rather an imperfection. Therefore even if a human gift were able to satisfy it perfectly, it would still be an imperfect gift because the need is an imperfection. But to need the good and perfect gift from God is a perfection; therefore the gift, which is the in and for itself, is also a perfect gift, because the need is a perfection." In fact there is no analogy between earthly need and the need for the gift: "earthly need is so far from illuminating [the need for the gift] by analogy that it obscures it instead." Earthly need or lack is always relative to a prior normative ideal and therefore derivative; it is what the ancients called a "privation," an absence of what should be. Need, by contrast, is a perfection: it constitutes an originary capability; not a capability dependent upon some prior constitution of the human being, but one through which the human being first becomes possible. Need is the first category, so to speak, through which to think human power. A paradox, then: the human is *enabled to be* through its need—something that cannot be said about any form of lack. Need points not to any deficiency relative to a prior norm, but to an excess of the gift over any capacity to receive it. Indeed, the being of the human being *is* this excess. Not only can the human being not appropriate its own being—since its being is gift—an essential task devolves upon human existence: that of tending to or preserving the condition of need. The inability to appropriate the gift due to its excess over the receptive powers of the self places the human being in a condition of need—ultimately, a need to respond to the gift, to "preserve" its excess.

However, need has its own phenomenological genesis in human life; it does not immediately determine human self-understanding. On the contrary: the first thing the human being encounters is its own "power and capability,"[21] something that manifests itself in the effort at knowledge—an effort whose ultimate expression lies in the effort at self-foundation. To be is first of all to relate to oneself as capable; the human access to its own capability is the first principle of the "old order of things." Need, therefore, becomes perceptible only on condition of a rupture from this immediate determination: "Before this need awakens in a human being there must have taken place a *great overturning*." Before need becomes apparent the human being must have undergone a detachment of itself from its own power—this is the great overturning. A condition of essential anguish. Need presupposes this de-adherence of the human being from its own capability. Outside of this need is simply buried under the project structure and, more precisely, under the effort at knowledge.

With the inception of need, however, it is not a question of simply jettisoning knowledge. In fact knowledge itself, conditioned and driven by doubt, maintains a secret association with the great overturning: "the whole of doubt's busy deliberations were humanity's first attempt at encountering [the great overturning]."[22] It is necessary to underscore that the great overturning does not simply refer to a particular event; it is rather a category, a structure, already operative in an epochal-historical way in the effort at knowledge. Doubt's busy deliberations were *humanity's* first attempt, epochally-historically, to grasp the unconditioned, that is, the non-apparent foundation of appearances. The effort at knowledge, conditioned and opened by doubt, constitutes the organizing principle of the "old order of things." Doubt, in its expression as the effort at knowledge, consists in the task of "penetrating everything that has preceded it" and in this way confronts the *given*. The given is its horizon. Doubt however thereby implicitly seeks the giving of the given, the true unconditioned. But this can be encountered only in the rupture from its own capability—only in this rupture is human capability not presupposed, but shows itself in its quality as something given. The movement of doubt is thus internalized. Doubt is inverted so as to become knowledge's *self-doubt*—in other words, doubt concerning the power of consciousness to found itself. Kierkegaard writes: "the untrue doubt doubts everything; the doubt that saves doubts only itself."

Self-doubt in this sense does not indicate a psychological state, but clarity about the impossibility of self-foundation.

The gift wounds human life by burdening it with an excess over any capability to internalize, appropriate or express it. Need thus arises, not out of a sense of lack, but out of the burden of an excess. How to express the gift, put it to use? Unlike earthly need (i.e., lack), need cannot be satisfied; it has no horizon of fulfillment. Yet need must not be understood as an insatiable *desire* for being as if, like *eros*, it would be the child of *poros* and *penia*. Need is not erotic: the need for the gift is not the desire for the gift. In need the gift is already completely realized (perfect), not the forever deferred term of its desire. The gift is not something *sought for*; it "comes down from above" and is always already there prior to, and as the condition of, its reception.

According to Kierkegaard the need that opens up with the rift in human life constitutes a fecund "new beginning," a beginning in which the human being "has no intermediary between God and himself since he is in possession of the condition that he cannot give himself since it is a gift from God."[23] The effort at knowledge, constituting the "old order of things," is the work of mediation *par excellence*. The human being comes about in this order as conquest of the past, as the assimilation of its conditions, and thus as the *outcome* of a project of self-appropriation. This project is in principle infinite—indeed, knowledge is a project constituted by an infinite desire-to-be. This order is overthrown in need, that is, in the detaching of the subject from its power to posit itself and so constitute the source of projects. The gift is given prior to any horizon of any thing given and in this way is immediate. Therefore it never becomes available for knowledge; knowledge comes essentially too late.

If the gift cannot be sought or appropriated, however, if it is an immediacy that wounds, nevertheless it can and must be tended to as such: "But since the condition [i.e. need] is itself a perfection, it must be cared for (*bevares*) as such, so that it is not divided up and scattered and acquires only a partial meaning."[24] To tend to and protect need, to prevent its occlusion in a project-oriented existence, emerges as the essential task of the human being in the order constituted by gift. It is the manner in which human existence becomes the site wherein the "first shoots of creation" irrupts. Tending to need, the human being is "born by means of and toward the order of truth." Need is the connection of the human being to its essential natality. The truth of human existence is not realized as knowledge, but as a tending to its condition of need. This task, which coincides with existence itself and so is infinite, consists of rooting out "wrath" (*Vrede*). In this regard Kierkegaard cites the text from James 1:20: "for the wrath of man does not put into effect the justice of God." Whenever the human being is separated from his own power and capability, wrath lies close by. Wrath: in other words *resentment*, the refusal of being, the refusal of the gift. Wrath would obliterate the condition of natality in the lamentation that it would be better not to have been born. To tend to and preserve the gift would be to live in a condition of "pliancy" (*Sagtmodighed*): to let the old order of truth go, to let go every attachment to lack, to see overturned all normalized conceptions of what counts as gift and what does not count—to regard one's existence *in toto* as gift, beyond all lack—that is the essential task.

3

Undergoing time: discourses on patience (1843–44)

Between 1843 and 1844 Kierkegaard wrote three discourses on patience, the most important of which is titled "To Gain One's Soul in Patience," from *Four Upbuilding Discourses* (1843). The discourses aim at an "inversion of thought and speech" vis-à-vis the theme of patience. Whereas patience normally signifies a comportment adopted by a self within a larger teleological context— patience is always "for the sake of" some other end—Kierkegaard thinks it as an essential, purely intrinsic attunement. Patience acquires its meaning solely for its power to bring about patience; one is patient in order to be patient. As will be seen, this withdrawal of patience from any teleological setting amounts to its "ontologization:" rather than being adopted by the self as a comportment necessary to accomplishment of its projects, patience signifies the attunement in which the self first comes to be. Patience is *that wherein* there is first a self; or, the self first "gains itself" in patience.

Normally, however, patience signifies something within the larger economy of the already existing self. Either it signifies the deferral of enjoyment necessary to secure the material "conditions of life"—the fisherman adopts patience as what is necessary for catching fish, for example—or it signifies a "virtue"—namely, one of the comportments necessary to the self's achievement of the "ultimate end-goal" of *eudaimonia* (human flourishing). Either way, patience gains its meaning from a larger project in which it is embedded. In the purely economic sense, patience can never be more than a contingent disposition, something manifest in that, with the achievement of the end-goal (catching fish, for example), patience gives way to enjoyment. The deferral of enjoyment is but a moment. In a virtue context, it is true, patience may acquire a more intrinsic meaning. Indeed, in the virtue context—canonically articulated in Aristotle's *Nicomachean Ethics*—all the virtues acquire a certain intrinsic value beyond their status as powers conducive to the achievement of ends: they are sought for, and exercised, in some measure as ends-in-themselves and not only as a means towards further ends. This is owing to their connection to *eudaimonia* which—although the "ultimate end-goal" of all human action—cannot be reduced to a determinate, finite goal. In a virtue context patience constitutes one of the dispositions necessarily implied in the *infinite project* of human flourishing. There would be no "good life" outside of the exercise of patience. Even so, patience would still be something exercised and adopted by a self already presupposed to exist, that is, to be in possession of itself.

Kierkegaard's withdrawal of patience from a teleological setting enacts a fundamental revaluation of temporality. Temporality does not coincide with the time opened up by the self's projects—its projecting itself out ahead of itself toward an end-goal—but with the movement by which the self undergoes its being. Patience in this sense signifies the impossibility of appropriating time; it gestures to a deferral, an impossibility for the self to coincide with itself, that is absolute.

The circle of patience

As indicated, Kierkegaard's discourse begins with a paradox: if patience is not a comportment adopted by the self but rather a comportment in which the self first comes to be, then who is the agent of patience? Can the self precede itself in being? Conversely, must not any activity of gaining, including the gaining of the self, presuppose an already constituted self? Kierkegaard formulates the paradox as follows:

> But if a person possesses his soul, he certainly does not need to gain it, and if he does not possess it, how then can he gain it, since the soul itself is presupposed as the ultimate condition in every acquiring, consequently also in gaining the soul. Could there be a possessing of such a kind that it would signify precisely the condition of being able to gain that same possessing?[1]

A circle: in patience one is to gain that which is the condition of any gaining. Therefore one must already have gained, as a condition of the gaining, that which is to be gained. How then could such a gaining ever begin?[2] How to enter this circle? Is this not a vicious circle?

In fact, the circle is only vicious on condition that one understands patience as an act-by-a-subject, that is, as a project. According to this understanding—which is the understanding both of common sense and a predominant philosophical tradition—the subject is original, foundation reality, and patience, just like any other act, is something contingent that, as such, can never attain to the status of an ultimate condition. The ultimate condition is the subject. Thus an act, always and essentially something conditioned, is conceived as originating in some inner power of the subject and always takes the form of *agere propter finem* (acting for an end-goal).[3] An act is a project inaugurated by the subject who dominates and constitutes the act, from beginning to end. If this understanding grounds one's approach to patience the paradox is insuperable.

Kierkegaard's discourse, however, does not treat patience as an act-by-a-subject. This makes for a novel development, an "inversion in thought and speech" with respect to the predominant tradition. In fact the problematic of the discourse, far from presupposing some substance-subject, aims to clarify the originary conditions in which the subject—the "soul" in the terms of the discourse—comes to be at all. And that is *in* patience. Patience precedes the subject as its ultimate—I will say "transcendental"—condition. In addition to this, Kierkegaard will say, patience qualifies as the essential work of the soul: the subject comes to be, "gains itself," as a modality of patience, as a "repetition" or immersion in this ultimate condition. Patience is the very "how," the way of being, of the subject: its "wherefrom" and its "whereto." As Kierkegaard himself indicates, there is a certain monstrosity to this thought insofar as what one gains in patience is simply patience itself—patience therefore without an end-goal or "why." To the usual understanding this dimension can only appear as the abyss of *futile labor*: laboring for the sake of laboring. Sisyphus.

The difficulty of this discourse—and this is one of Kierkegaard's most difficult discourses—is to understand what patience could signify, not as an act, but as the ultimate in-which of the subject. In addition, it will be essential to grasp how patience, though presented as the essential work of the soul, is neither an action nor a project. Finally, what could patience be as filling out the meaning of the being of the soul, as constituting its horizon, as the ultimate for-the-sake-of-which of its existence? To say therefore that the subject exists in, for and through patience? Why patience?

A pre-indication about the direction of this problematic can be gleaned from reflection on the everyday circumstances of patience: patience in the pre-philosophical sense concerns a relation to *temporality* and, in particular, it suggests something unwanted, an *undergoing*. Indeed, the Danish word for patience (*Taalmodigheden*), similar to its English equivalent, contains the root idea of bearing up under, tolerating, or undergoing (*at taale*). Kierkegaard retrieves these traits from the everyday experience of patience and elevates them to the status of ultimate conditions. In so doing he raises the problem of an originary temporality to which the soul is subject—a temporality, therefore, that is fundamentally undergone. The work of patience will then appear as an immersion in such temporality: in *becoming temporal* the soul would gain itself.

The determinations of soul

Kierkegaard's first task in this discourse is to attack the notion of a substance-subject that rules much of Western thought, particularly its various theories of action. In order to effect this desubstantialization, he presents the soul—not according to a logic of entities—but as a "contradiction." He writes: the "soul is therefore in contradiction and is self-contradiction." He elaborates: the "soul is a self-contradiction between the internal and the external, the temporal and the eternal. It is a self-contradiction, because wanting to express the contradiction within itself is precisely what makes it what it is."[4] This appeal to contradiction as constitutive of the soul's reality is only intelligible in light of the Hegelian developments in logic according to which logic is, most basically, not the logic of *entities*—as the tradition of Aristotle would have it—but a *phenomeno*-logic, the logic of consciousness. According to Hegel's famous formulation for consciousness one must say that "it is what it is not and it is not what it is." Consciousness in itself expresses a contradiction. But this means: consciousness is always other than itself, simultaneously absent and present to itself: it is always *becoming*. Becoming requires the simultaneity of being and not-being, that is, contradiction. And not only this, but consciousness knows itself *as* in becoming; it is a becoming for-itself. Or, as Kierkegaard puts it, the soul is not only a contradiction but a "self-contradiction," that is, it is aware of its own contradictory nature, of the manner in which it is ever in a state of becoming, and it makes an effort to express that.

Hence to call the soul a "contradiction" says nothing other, initially, than that the soul is not a thing and, hence, that the logic of entities—governed by the law of non-contradiction—cannot capture its reality. In Kierkegaard's terms it is only the "external" (the realm of things) that is governed by the law of non-contradiction. The soul has its reality, however, in the "internal," the dimension of becoming and self-relation. But if the soul is in this way a contradiction, this serves immediately to banish the aporia that a soul cannot both gain itself and possess itself at the same time. If, namely, a soul's very reality is contradiction, if it always both is and is not, then it *can* simultaneously be and not be itself, possess itself and gain itself. It can become itself.

Kierkegaard, however, tracks down the notion of a substance-subject finally to a certain presupposed understanding of temporality: "more closely defined, it was actually temporality that made it impossible to possess and to gain the external simultaneously, because that which is in the moment either is or is not, and if it is, then it is not gained, and if it is gained, then it is not."[5] This understanding of temporality treats the moment—the "now"—as if it were just another entity and, consequently, as governed by an exclusionary relation between being and non-being, presence and absence. It either is or it is not. However, this merely "external" or thingly conception of temporality cannot capture the temporality of the soul's "internal" relation to itself in becoming. "Internally" the soul does not just *have* time, but it is thoroughly temporal in the sense that the soul's relation to itself is constituted temporally. Between the soul and itself there is a temporality not reducible to thingly or external temporality.

To elaborate this dimension of internal temporality Kierkegaard invokes the category of "the eternal." The appeal to the eternal in this discourse, however, is somewhat cursory.[6] Kierkegaard invokes the eternal as the contradictory pole to the temporal: hence the being of the soul may also be stated as "a contradiction between the temporal and the eternal."[7] It is not immediately obvious what this means, however. In particular, what precise understanding of temporality is invoked here? It cannot be the flattened, thingly conception of temporality, since Kierkegaard has already argued that this "external" sense of time does not apply to the "internal" time of the soul.

Nor would it be of any help to say that the soul's internal time is somehow composed out of the contradictory elements of thingly time and eternity.

In any case, the discourse elaborates another, deeper contradiction that emerges in the soul's relation to the eternal. Kierkegaard sketches his concept of the eternal—also referred to as "the eternal essence," or God—with a few quick strokes: "In the eternal there is no ... self-contradiction, but not because it, like the temporal, either is or is not, but because it is."[8] The eternal is being without a relation to non-being, that is, necessary being. The eternal cannot not be. To think the being of God through this idea of the eternal is to reproduce classical ontotheology. However, that is not Kierkegaard's concern here, where it is a question of setting forth the in-principle possibility of the soul's gaining itself. The question is: how does the soul, which is not eternal, relate to the eternal? How does the soul relate to necessary being, to being that cannot not be? How does this help clarify an internal temporal capable of supporting the soul's gaining of itself?

It is here where Kierkegaard's analysis takes a novel turn in elaborating a contradiction that emerges in the soul's very relation to the eternal. The key passage is the following: "the eternal is nothing that be either possessed or gained, but is a possession (*et Eiet*) that can no more be gained than lost."[9] The soul, in other words, relates to the eternal in a contradictory mode: it possesses it without possessing it. And because this relation is wholly internal—that is, the eternal is nothing over against the soul, but implicated in the soul's relation to itself—the same can be said in relation to the soul's being: it possesses itself without possessing itself. One could say it *is possessed of self*. By way of its relation to the eternal, consequently, the soul is thrust into the contradictory position that it cannot possess its ownmost proper being; and, further, since it is neither possible to possess or to lose the eternal, the soul can neither possess nor lose itself. Its own being clings to the self in such a way that it cannot rid itself of itself. This is the concrete contradiction, the double bind, that constitutes the ultimate condition in which the soul is to gain itself: to the extent that it does not possess itself, the soul can *gain* itself; and to the extent that it nevertheless does possess itself, it can gain *itself*. The ambiguity of the soul's relation to the eternal thus constitutes the condition of the possibility of the soul's gaining itself: were the soul not originally possessed of self, always already in a relation to itself, it could not gain itself; were it not just as originally marked by difference, a difference legible in its fundamental passivity vis-à-vis itself, it could not gain itself.

The full import of Kierkegaard's discourse on patience now becomes clearer: he thinks through this unique structure—that the soul can neither appropriate itself nor rid itself of itself—in relation to the problem of internal time. Precisely by way of its relation to eternity, *not being able not to be*, an essential rift is created between the soul and itself, a rift from which to think originary time as the time of patience. The rift between the soul and itself signifies that the soul is not present at its own origin, that it does not inaugurate itself.

Kierkegaard's discourse at this point must be read against the grain of the idealist account of the self as that which posits itself. According to the famous Fichtean analysis a self only *is* as a positing-of-self, as a possessing of self. With infinite speed, as it were, the self is there at itself, already in command of itself. There is nothing prior to the self's having a grip on itself: this instant of self-gripping *is* the self. The very concept of the self here is that of what is free from necessity, from any past, the concept of that which is always launching itself anew.[10] The Fichtean self, in this way defined by its self-creation, is essentially impatient. Where reality bears down upon the self in its necessity it is a mere "obstacle" (*Anstoss*) to be surmounted.

To place patience at the origin, in this context, is to indicate the structure of an always-prior delay or deferral, within which the soul can gain itself. Kierkegaard's discourse here retrieves and radicalizes—"transcendentalizes"—an element intrinsic to patience in its everyday sense: that of waiting, or of temporal delay. To transcendentalize this trait means to conceive temporality itself through a structure of delay. However, this is not to be thought as a merely provisional moment of a process. Delay in the transcendental sense at issue cannot be thought in terms of a durational quantity or a stretch of time. In the strict sense patience makes no reference to any length of time at all, neither long nor short.[11] To introduce a durational quantity would be to introduce "externality" back into the "internal" event of genesis. Time itself irrupts in an instant neither long nor short—but in any case, it irrupts carrying with it insurmountable, unconditional delay. This delay signifies the soul's in-principle inability to get a hold on itself, to seize itself in its origin: which is precisely the condition of a gaining of itself as an essential work.

But until now Kierkegaard's discourse has only considered the conditions for the possibility of the soul's gaining itself. It has raised a "transcendental" problematic. It has yet to clarify this gaining as a concrete economy. For one thing, the soul always already finds itself immersed in a world and thereby, Kierkegaard will say, possessed by the world. The way will have to be clarified, therefore, by which the soul gains itself *from* the world before one can clarify how patience is the *essential* labor of the soul. The full statement of the economy of gaining will be: the soul gains itself, if it does, "from God, away from the world, through [itself]."

The project of self-possession

Now that that in-principle possibility of the soul's gaining of itself has been clarified, the discourse turns to an elaboration of the economy of gaining. The Danish word *erhverve* (to gain or acquire), indeed, invokes the specifically economic structures of labor, exchange, and possession. The question is: through what kind of labor and what sort of exchange does the soul acquire itself (if it does)? And what does it mean for the soul to possess itself? However, in raising this problematic Kierkegaard is alive to a certain risk: that of importing the categories of the "external" economy to the "internal" economy of the soul. Kierkegaard's analysis thus begins with a critique of the external economy and the values organizing it.

Unlike Marx's analysis of political economy, Kierkegaard's critique is hardly systematic, but it does seek to be an in-principle critique of a set of pseudo-values, values that constitute the economic system organized around the commodity. In this regard, the premier "external" value the discourse wishes to criticize is that of possession itself. In a surprising convergence with Marx, Kierkegaard writes: "the external and the temporal becomes what it is supposed to be *only when no one possesses it at all*, or when it has become a matter of indifference."[12] In the external and temporal realm, the realm of the commodity, possession reveals itself as an illusory value. The commodity can be possessed only "as the contingent, as that which can decrease, increase, be lost, be won without one's [mode of] possession being essentially altered."[13] What structures commodity possession is the contingency of fortune (*Lykke*): the commodity gains and loses value according to laws that fundamentally have nothing to do with the commodity "in itself"—Marx would say the commodity acquires "exchange value." Moreover, the real relation to the commodity is the inverse of what it seems to be: it is that the commodity, rather than being possessed, instead possesses the possessor. However, this being-possessed by that which one takes oneself to possess, by the commodity, is hidden from the possessor himself. The reversal occurs behind his back, as it were, as the very "cunning" of the commodity.

This illusion, though hardly recognized in the external world, is pernicious insofar as it tacitly underlies accounts of what it means to gain one's soul, or to possess oneself. It functions, to be specific, as the presupposition of what may be called "the project of self-possession." This is the idea that the soul can *produce itself* through its activity, that it can have itself at its disposal, a finished thing—like the commodity. The external economy is indeed organized around the production of value, values which turn out to be illusory. The economy of patience, Kierkegaard will say, is structured inversely around the loss of apparent values: "There is no talk here about adding something to the soul, but about taking something from it, that is, something that is only apparently possessed." Among these apparent values to be lost is the notion that the soul must gain itself in actions aiming at an end-goal, that is to say, must produce itself. This occurs when the soul projects itself—its "accomplished" self—as the end-goal of its striving. The economy of patience, Kierkegaard will say, is not organized around an end-goal because it is not constituted in terms of productive activity. The following formula, invoked several times by Kierkegaard, pertains to it: "we know not what we shall become."

Kierkegaard traces the birth of the inverted world to the beginning, the condition of immediacy. He writes: "Human beings are closest to that which they seek—to posses the world—in their first moment, when their soul is lost in [the world] and possesses the world in itself, the way that a wave possesses the unrest of the sea and depths of the abyss in itself."[14] Thus begins the inverted or false consciousness: in the moment of immersion in the plenitude of being, a condition of non-differentiation—of infancy, immediacy—human beings are already at the goal which they come to project forward, by a supreme anachronism, as the object of their striving. To bathe in the plenitude of being, what Freud would call the "oceanic," is adopted as the end-goal of striving, the very criterion of self-possession. And in the condition of immediacy the soul is notably infinite: it exists as non-differentiated from the "infinity in the life of the world."[15] Here the soul possesses itself as the world and the world as itself.

However, the moment of immediacy—which persists as a structural moment in all consciousness—is in fact always already broken, traversed by a counter-pull toward finitude. Kierkegaard says: "[the soul in immediacy] has an intimation (*fornemmer*) of a counter-force that does not follow along with the movements of the life of the world."[16] Something prevents the soul from bathing in infinitude. Kierkegaard fixes this counter-force more categorically in a new formula for the being of the soul: "[the soul] is [in this moment] the infinity of the life of the world in its *difference from itself*."[17] An element of difference, or negation, always already marks the soul, subjecting it to a counter-pull, blocking its full immersion in being, making it finite.

Now Kierkegaard traces the birth of an illusory world of values to this exact point: the moment at which the soul senses the counter-pull of negation upon its being. In face of this erosion in being, a strategy is born: the effort to master the negation. He writes: "If the soul is now to gain the world, it must master this unrest [of the negative], until it again disappears as a wave in the movements of the life of the world."[18] The fecund idea at the source of a world of illusory values, therefore, is that negation can be negated. The soul interprets the negative counter-pull as a contingency, as a lack in its being that therefore can be supplemented. *Thus arises the project of self-constitution:* the soul projects, as an ideal focal point to organize its activity, its "fulfilled" self, its possessed self. It aims to produce itself through its own activity and have itself at its disposal.

Meanwhile, as it pursues the effort to master the negation suppurating at its core, the soul exists only "outside itself" (*uden for sig*), exterior to itself. All the soul's labor is defined by its exteriority. Remaining in the relation of exteriority toward the world—which is to say, within the horizon in which the world appears as a set of possessable commodities—the soul makes a futile effort to re-interiorize the world, to take it into the zone of what is proper to it. Within this project, patience may indeed be necessary as a strategy, but it can ever only be contingently necessary.

The attempt on the part of the soul to constitute itself by way of "productive labor" is no more than a "despairing effort to secure itself."[19] To gain itself authentically another economy must be engaged—indeed, an economy defined in terms, not of increase and gain, but rather of subtraction of loss. At stake will be unlearning the modalities of possession derived from the world of the commodity, disengaging from oceanic immersion, and learning a whole new manner of self-possession, a mode of possessing constituted in terms of a non-possession of self. Patience is here engaged, not contingently, but *essentially*.

This dynamic is not identical to the strategy of renunciation, but is rather a deepening in the soul's very condition: that is, in the suppurating difference at its heart. The true gaining will be defined in terms of a letting the "infinitude of the life of the world *in its difference from itself*" become more and more salient. This coincides with the soul's "weaving itself into" (*spinder sig ind*) its own finitude. And here patience emerges as the essential labor of the human being.

Patience as repetition

When, then, *is* the work of patience? As already underscored, to grasp the work of patience, it is necessary to withdraw it from any moral-pragmatic register. Morally-pragmatically patience signifies a *contingently* adopted comportment within a larger telic order of actions ordained to end-goals. One exercises patience *in-order-to*, as a means conducive to the attainment of a projected end-goal. The whole sense and meaning of patience, its whole justification, lay in something beyond patience itself, namely in the value of the projected end-goal—even and especially if that end-goal is one's "authentic self." Thus, in a moral-pragmatic horizon, patience is "a third thing" (*noget Tredie*), something in addition to the one who acts and that for which he acts. It is a means employed by the one who strives, a tool to be used in the service of the attainment of the end-goal. Morally-pragmatically, patience can never be unconditionally necessary. Whether patience is necessary or not, and the extent to which it might be recommended, is dictated by the contingent character of the world, "all according to fortune." Patience in this context is praised as a virtue (*Sjelstyrke*), but it would be better, "in a purely human sense," if patience were not required.

By considering patience as the one essential work, the work by which a person "gains one's soul," Kierkegaard's discourse thus removes it from any larger telic order. What is one supposed to gain in patience? Nothing other than patience. And how is one supposed to gain it? In patience. In order to gain patience, therefore, patience is necessary; or, one must have patience to have patience. Again, a circle. Drawing upon the transcendental language of the condition and the conditioned, Kierkegaard is careful to secure a proper understanding of this circle: "*In patience.* The expression does not say by means of or with reference to patience, but 'in' patience, indicating thereby that the condition stands in a unique relation to the conditioned."[20] The condition, to be more exact, is identical to that which it conditions: "the condition is also the object and does not depend upon anything external." This indicates that patience is a "becoming within its own presupposition,"[21] a process constituting its own originary possibility—what Kierkegaard will call a "redoubling repetition" (*fordoblende Gjentagelse*). Patience is thus simultaneously that which conditions the soul in its very possibility and a work of that soul—it is both condition and conditioned.

How, then, can patience be described as a work? What is needed is to clarify the very inception of patience, that is, how patience *breaks through* into human existence prior to, and as the condition of, a soul gaining itself in relation. To clarify the inbreaking of patience—and here what is at issue is patience in its transcendental sense, patience as the sense of insurmountable delay the soul undergoes in relation to itself—is at the same time to clarify the ultimate condition of the soul's gaining itself. The breakthrough of patience, the coming upon the soul of patience, is the breakthrough of the soul to itself, the becoming available for a soul to gain itself. The following passage contains the central dynamic: "Thus in the first moment the human being is . . . lost in the life of the world. But in the same moment he is different from the world and he senses (*fornemmer*) a counter-striving that does not follow the movements of the life of the world. If he now wants to gain the world, he must master this disquiet until once again . . . he vanishes in the life of the world . . . However, if he wants to gain his soul, he must allow this counter-striving to stand out more and more and therein gain his soul. For his soul is precisely this difference: the infinitude in the life of the world in its difference from itself.[22]" Already in the situation of oceanic immersion, of bathing in the plenitude of being—a moment that persists in human existence—a counterforce of resistance breaks in and makes itself felt. Something prevents the soul from being lost in its enjoyment of being. The soul gains access to itself only on condition that this disruptive mood, this patience, makes itself felt. The work of patience is to allow this mood to break in more and more, to cede to it greater and greater place. The work of impatience, by contrast, is the effort to master this disquiet, to master the negation or difference breaking out at its core. Impatience is the soul's effort to negate the negation, to reestablish itself within the plenitude of being, to re-inhabit the plane of infinitude.

The structure of patience as a work now becomes clear: it is not originally a doing, not an act, but an un-doing or an allowing. In acting the soul posits itself, modifies itself with a new determination, gains new powers; in patience, on the other hand, the soul adds nothing to itself, something is rather *subtracted*. Kierkegaard writes: "There is no talk [with respect to patience] of adding something to the soul, but rather of subtracting something from it, that is, something that it only apparently possessed."[23] The gaining of the soul coincides with a losing: "[in patience the soul] can only gain by losing" (*kun erhverve ved at tabe*).[24] In patience the soul gains itself only by being un-done, de-constituted, stripped of what it only apparently possesses. The sense of finitude, breaking into the realm of its attachments, is the acid that strips the soul of its founding illusion—namely, its illusion of possessing itself.

Patience as an "act" is thus non-resistance to the counter-force that deprives the soul of its most intimate attachment to life: its (apparent) identity with the infinitude of the life of the world. The breaking of this attachment, this most intimate event, is the condition of the soul's gaining of itself—*if*, that is, it can withstand the rupture, if it can avoid the effort to re-master the negation, if it can be patient.

The breaking of the soul's immediate attachment to life and to its infinitude, then, is the originary condition for a work of gaining. But this does not yet describe the process of gaining itself. How does it unfold? Kierkegaard's answer: by and as a *repetition*. The work of patience is a "redoubling repetition" (*fordoblende Gjentagelse*). By "repetition" Kierkegaard indicates something precise: it describes a becoming in which "the condition stands in a unique relation to the conditioned."[25] The condition, namely, redoubles itself as the conditioned, forming a relation of identity. What enables the becoming (the condition) doubles as what the becoming brings about (the conditioned). A repetition is thus "a becoming within its own presupposition,"[26] an unfolding from out of its own origin. It is a becoming with no other end-goal than its own unfolding, aiming at nothing other than its own re-inception. It is a becoming purely immanent to itself, blossoming under its own energy. It should be clear that, even if an act can be repeated by a subject ad infinitum, an act could never be a repetition, because the structure of an act presupposes a split between condition and conditioned—namely between the act and that toward which it acts.[27]

The work of patience, the gaining of the soul, is a repetition. This means: patience enables patience; or, it takes patience to have patience. There is a strict circle here in which patience is both the condition of the gaining and what is gained: "In this gaining the condition is also the object and does not depend upon anything external. Therefore the condition, when it has served for the gaining, remains as the thing gained."[28] Obviously there is a paradox of origin with respect to this circle, making it seem impossible to enter into, insofar as one must *always already have* patience in order to become patient.

The seeming impossibility, however, is only apparent: it is a function of still thinking of patience as an act separable from, and inaugurated by, a subject—as though the soul would constitute the origin of a gaining. As indicated, however, patience is not originally an act inaugurated by the subject, but the in-breaking of a mood, the sense of finitude coming upon one, which irrupts in the soul's break from its immediate connection to the infinitude of life in which it had hitherto bathed. The soul does not inaugurate its own rupture of the immediate connection to life; this is an event coming upon the soul. By virtue of this event, however, the soul is already "in" patience, already invested with the condition to gain patience (and itself). The in-breaking of patience, therefore, is the setting of the soul into the circle of patience, the soul's originary enablement to undertake patience as a work—which is to say, to become itself. Thus the soul does not stand at the inception of its own becoming. It becomes itself within the repetition of the event of rupture, that is, within the immanent unfolding of the mood of finitude.

A repetition may be described as a self-intensifying becoming, or a becoming absorbed in its own condition. This is how Kierkegaard describes repetition:

> This is not about conquering, chasing after or grasping something, but about becoming stiller and stiller ... because what is to be gained is in patience—not hidden inside it, as if it were a matter of patiently peeling away the layers of patience in order to find [the soul] at its core, but inside it in the sense that it is into patience itself that the soul, in patience, spins itself—and thereby gains patience and its soul.

Actually, repetition as a self-intensifying becoming is a regular phenomenon attending moods: anxiety blooms, for example, in anxiety. Anxiety unfolds from out of itself as a being anxious about being anxious; it grows through its own immanent force. So too patience. In a way, it's simple: "when the one who is gaining himself is simply patient then patience grows in him."[29] The soul becomes patient—and thereby becomes itself—in simply allowing it to blossom. This is not a doing, but a ceasing to do, a becoming "stiller and stiller."[30] In patience the soul gains itself through allowing itself to sink deeper into the sense of finitude: that letting-happen is the work of patience.

Patience as repetition thus cannot be equated with the project of patience because this would presuppose, again, a purely active relation to one's finitude: namely, reducing finitude to an achievable state, a representable end-goal. No program or set of techniques can be followed so as to become patient or finite. In this sense there is nothing "finite" about finitude. Becoming patient cannot signify "to start acting patiently" as though one, for example, were starting a diet. No new program of life is at issue, no new end-goal at stake. What is rather at stake is entering into a becoming in which one "does not know what we shall become." There is no other goal in becoming patient than becoming patient.

Patience and the signification of time: Anna

The problematic of patience, then, is first of all a transcendental one clarifying the conditions in which the soul gains itself. Patience is a significant term in this regard insofar as it invokes not only an event of undergoing, but a relation to time. In conclusion, therefore, what must be considered is the new signification Kierkegaard's discourse gives to temporality starting from and in terms of this problematic. What does time mean for the patient one? What is the sense of time?

Temporality is normally defined by project structure: the present gains its meaning in relation to a projected end-goal that has been retrieved from a past or latent possibility. Temporality is invested with a fundamental for-the-sake-of-which, an orienting point from which to gauge what "now" means. Indeed, Kierkegaard's discourses on "expectancy" also seem to be inscribed in this understanding of time: expectancy and the future, he said, belong essentially together. Therefore the person of faith is oriented wholly to the future; the present gains its meaning through the tension of this expectation.

The discourses on patience, by contrast, are anti-teleological to their core. Just where one might expect the elaboration of the project form—in the notion of gaining—Kierkegaard substitutes the idea of repetition. A repetition is an immersion in a condition of which one is *not* the author, a condition precisely disengaged from a telic meaning. "Transcendental" patience signifies the rupturing of the immediate connection of life, an event that leaves the soul in the state of "not knowing what we shall become." Patience is the labor of immersing oneself in that, of resisting the world of pseudo-values that arises when one takes that rupture to be a masterable form of negation.

In a certain way, then, in patience time comes to lose signification. Where am I headed? Where am I at now? In face of the work of patience these questions cease to be fundamental. In this sense Kierkegaard can describe the work of patience as one of "translating oneself into eternity" (*oversætter sig i Evigheden*). This should not confuse. The eternal is not some separate region of being outside of time. On the contrary, the eternal is accessed in the soul's relation to itself, in its inexpungible being-possessed-of-self. This relation was formed prior to, and as the condition of, any exercise of self and thus "eternally" enacted. Patience, bypassing the more familiar self of the project, allows this "deeper" self, a self disengaged from projects, to come to the fore. This is the self *before* meaning. And yet patience does not commit the self to sheer meaninglessness either.

Kierkegaard takes up the relation between patience and meaning in a discourse from 1844 titled "Patience in Expectancy." The discourse mediates on the biblical figure of Anna from Luke 2. Anna, a "prophet" awaiting the Messiah, "is in the strictness and noblest sense: the expectant one."[31] And the precise object of Anna's expectancy is "the fullness of time,"[32] the appearance of the Messiah. Prior to the appearance of the child Jesus her relation toward time was characterized by "patience in expectancy." Indeed, though Kierkegaard has disentangled the attunements in prior discourses, the discourse on Anna makes it clear that, concretely, expectancy always and essentially is correlated with patience: one waits upon an expected future.

It is critically important, however, to make clear how patience and expectancy relate to each other. In particular what must be avoided is any inscription of the attunement of patient-expectation within a teleological framework. It could appear that Anna has organized her existence, her sense of time, around a future representation, the object of her expectancy, the appearance of the one in whom the fullness of time will be realized. And she is most definitely waiting upon this concrete event, to see it "with her own eyes." But if indeed her existence was organized around a concrete future event, patience would only be incumbent upon her *so long as* the fulfillment was delayed; patience would be exercised, perhaps as a sign of her fortitude, in the name of an ultimate for-the-sake-of-which, an ultimate end-goal. Upon the realization of that end-goal, expectancy would cease, just as patience. In other words, patient-expectancy would again be a contingently adopted "third thing," subordinate to the moment of realization, rather than the essential work by which one gains one's soul. How, then, to think the attunement of patience-in-expectancy in a way that sufficiently accounts for the radical meaning Kierkegaard has given patience?

For Anna, indeed, the object of fulfillment comes to pass on the temporal plane. She witnesses time fulfilled in the presentation of the child Jesus of Nazareth at the temple; her expectation is therefore not disappointed. "But," Kierkegaard asks, "in what sense was she not deceived?"[33] A decisive question. Suppose she never lived to see the moment, what then? "Can Anna be deceived in her expectancy; can the fulfillment come too late?"[34] This is an in-principle question seeking the essential structure underlying Anna's orientation toward time. For Kierkegaard she was not deceived in her expectation—*not*, as one might expect, because she lived to see its fulfillment—but only because her orientation toward temporal fulfillment contained, as it were, an element of indifference toward fulfillment and non-fulfillment. In a decisive passage Kierkegaard writes: "And even if [the fulfillment] had failed to come, she still would not have been deceived. The fulfillment came; in the same moment ... [Anna] desires only to wander away from there (*vandre bort herfra*), that is, not to remain with the fulfillment, but in another sense to enter into the fulfillment."[35]

Indicated in this depiction of Anna is an attunement toward time characterized by an essential *wandering* in which the meaning of time is detached from any temporal event of fulfillment *or* non-fulfillment, and in general from any representable future. The sense of time, of the present moment, is not here founded upon the tension between the not-yet of the present, defined by its lack, and the anticipated fulfillment in the future. Anna recognizes an excess of time to any moment of fulfillment—and thereby her attunement is one of essential patience and essential expectancy. It is as though time itself promised something beyond any anticipated end-goals, beyond any projects. What Anna lets go of is the ideal of fulfilled or complete time: not even the "fullness of time" could complete time! On the other hand, this letting-go of the moment of fulfillment is the only way to enter into time completely. Anna expresses the sense that time is complete in its very incompleteness, or incomplete in its very completeness. Her sense of time, her patience-in-expectancy, is thereby detached from any telic meaning, that is, committed to an essential wandering.

4

Human lack: to need God is a human being's highest perfection (1844)

Kierkegaard's first discourse from his 1844 *Four Upbuilding Discourses*, titled "To Need God is a Human Being's Highest Perfection," states the ontological problem at stake in all of the discourses in the most categorical way. At issue is human power or capability (*Formaaen*). According to a trajectory in Western thought, which Kierkegaard here appropriates, the idea of perfection is thought in terms of a *power to be*. To be "perfect" (*perfectus*) is not to conform to some ideal type, nor to be able to serve as a pre-established norm, but rather to be capable. God, for example, is perfect insofar as God has his being entirely through himself, on his own basis.

Spinoza extended this thought in the notion that all beings are perfect—or "real"—to the extent that they constitute in themselves a fundamental power to persist in being (the *conatus*).[1] The concept of perfection at stake in this discourse, similarly, needs to be explicated through an *active power* capable of increasing being. To speak of the "human being's highest perfection," as Kierkegaard does, is to ask about that ontological power—the capability to be—in its specifically human modality. How is the fundamental ontological power inflected across human existence? Where is it felt, mobilized, effective?

Kierkegaard's discourse takes up the questions in relation to a fundamental topos of Western thought: self-knowledge. "To know oneself" would be to come to understand oneself in relation to the capability to be, the originative ontological power.

As the discourse's title already indicates, however, Kierkegaard pursues a certain counter-thought: the highest perfection of a human being, the point at which the human is most capable, is located in its fundamental *need*, that is, in its lack of capability. In this we discern again the "inversion of thought and speech" that is always at the heart of the edifying writings. The highest perfection of a human being, Kierkegaard writes, is that "he is capable of nothing, nothing at all."[2]

The thought however is perhaps familiar, all too familiar. Does it not correspond to the strategy, denounced by Spinoza as much as Nietzsche, to diminish the human being in favor of a supreme being? Does it not invoke the nihilistic turn of life against life, a desperate strategy on the part of the human being to mobilize the energies of resentment? Or perhaps it is a dialectical thought: the human *recognition* of its fundamental powerlessness is already in itself a transmuted form of power? It is none of these. The discourse fights its way through various misunderstandings to uncover a power of affirmation that neither rests in nor excludes human capability. The ruling counter-thought that it pursues is that the whole dimension of human need, what would otherwise be understood through categories of lack, is to be read for a contrary sense.

Economizing need, isolating capacity

The preamble to Kierkegaard's discourse is a meditation on the common sense understanding of need: "With respect to the earthly, one needs little, and to the degree one needs less, the more perfect one is."[3] As Kierkegaard alludes, this proverb ultimately finds its justification in an ontology of Stoic inspiration: the perfection of the gods consists in precisely their absence of need and, though the human being remains finite and mortal, he can achieve a divine-like *ataraxia* through the strategic minimization of desires. In the sumptuous banquet envisioned by Epictetus, for example, a good strategy would be to wait patiently for the food to come around and take a moderate portion; an even better, more divine strategy would be to take nothing at all—not to *need* to take anything.

The sphere of need, though absolutely inescapable, is problematic for human beings insofar as, through its neediness, life is immersed in a matrix of forces beyond its control: the need for nourishment, shelter, money, fame, good health—all of these, so fundamental to human thriving, nevertheless follow laws of increase and decrease that escape human capability. Human existence is, on the one hand, thoroughly constituted by its needs and desires; but on the other hand, the worldly context of this desire—the cosmos—is governed by indifferent necessity. The cosmos doesn't care if human beings fulfill their desires. The position of the human being in the cosmos, then, is in a certain sense impossible; non-fulfillment, thwarted desire, is its implacable horizon.

The Stoic strategy, however, is to isolate the domain of real human capability, which means making a distinction between "what is up to us" and "what is not up to us."[4] The strategic significance of this distinction is clear: in relation to what is up to us, we always retain a basic, radical capability. The forces of necessity ruling the kaleidoscopic domain of needs have no essential bearing on the radical capability supporting human life: the power of *nous*. Through *nous* the human being remains in principle detachable from the domain of needs: the cosmos is in principle powerless to dictate to us our self-understanding, the modality of our response to its deprivations. In marking and re-marking the distinction between what is in our power and what is not in our power human beings can establish themselves through themselves, through a principle internal to their own being, and effectively deflect the "external" order of necessity. Need can be strategically minimized, human capability increased. Human beings can actively cultivate a power to do without, to adapt, to pare down to the essentials, and to achieve perspective on the domain of real being: the cosmos as a whole.[5] However, human capability is isolated and defined, it is extraordinary how little human beings can get by with, what they can endure, and still retain their integrity as persons. The Stoic thought is to celebrate the human as a fundamental power of resistance to an indifferent cosmos; one can even learn to enjoy non-fulfillment!

If Kierkegaard's discourse will speak of human need, and speak of it precisely as a perfection, it will not be in order to belittle human capability. It will solely be a question of whether the human being is thereby grasped with sufficient radicality. And in particular it will be a question of whether or not the human being is capable of "self-overcoming" (*at overvinde sig selv*). Nothing less than that. A capability, unless it is wholly imaginary, necessarily has reference to some force of resistance: "if a capability is really to be one, it must of course have opposition, for that which has no opposition is either almighty or imaginary."[6] In relation to the human, then, what resists the human? With this question Kierkegaard raises the genuinely ontological problem of capability: upon what is capability itself founded? What makes the human capable of being capable?

The human

The discourse asks: "But what is a human being?"[7] Answer: the being capable of undergoing its own nihilation (*Tilintetgjørelse*), for in his "nihilation he has his truth."[8] Except it won't be precisely a capability exercised *by which* one undergoes one's own annihilation; rather, it will be in the annihilation itself that the human being is invested with capability. The experience of nihilation will not be referred to any "external" power or force such that the human would encounter its own relative diminishment in face of a vaster reality. Nor is this encounter framed by Kierkegaard in terms of the encounter with one's ownmost impossibility to be, that is, in terms of one's being-towards-death. Death, faced authentically or not, is not that wherein one encounters nothingness. The human encounters its own nihilation, its own truth, solely in the encounter with an absolute incapacity it undergoes with respect to its own being: the experience of the impossibility on the part of the human being to break out of its being, to overcome itself. Overcoming oneself is the sole definition, the ontologically proper definition of power, that is, of being.

In the exclusive problem of self-overcoming, then, one perceives the novelty of Kierkegaard's discourse vis-à-vis dominant traditions—from Stoicism to Descartes to various idealisms—in which self-consciousness is grasped in a distinctive, self-founding role. Is self-consciousness a radical beginning, resting upon and arising in being through its own capability? Discourses characterized as "humanist," whether philosophical or theological, have always found in the autonomous powers of consciousness the marks by which to declare the human being as the "most glorious creation." In Kant, of course, autonomy becomes the "highest principle" of morality. Through the autonomy of consciousness the human being is capable of not merely acting according to laws, but in fact of acting in terms of its own conception of law—that is, consciousness realizes its power in freedom, in *spontaneity* vis-à-vis "external" determinants of the natural order. The truth of the human lies in its spontaneity, its power precisely to inaugurate a new sequence, a moral sequence, not resting in the automaticity of natural determinants.

Kierkegaard's discourse, not unlike Nietzsche, comes at the end of this philosophical trajectory. Recapitulating it, he asks: "does not the eye aim its arrow every time passion and desire tighten the bowstring, does not the hand grasp outward, is not his arm stretched out, and is not his ingenuity all-conquering?"[9] In the merest act of looking, in the outstretching of the arm, is expressed a fundamental "I Can." Through the I Can the human is capable of *grasping* the world; this is the source of all human activity, whether theoretical or practical. Kierkegaard's discourse, however, coincides with Spinoza's preemptive strike at this account: the eye that intends and the hand that grasps—in fact all the "movements of his soul"—transpire in strict accordance with "the way the world plucks its strings."[10] The intentionality relation is reversed. The human being always finds itself "in the hands of inexplicable moods," and not just by coincidence, but essentially.

It is in *affectivity*, in other words, that the springs of action are to be found, and affects are a function of the human being's immersion in fundamentally opaque powers, powers resistant to the penetration of the eye. Like Spinoza, Kierkegaard reverses the relation between freedom and thought as spontaneity and desire. To be free, to realize concretely the I Can, is to act on the strength of a desire—a desire, however, that freedom itself has not given itself. Desires are functions of the human cathexis into the world. Consciousness does not endow itself with its own moods, with its fundamental drives, and these are the radical sources of activity. There is an experience of pseudo-freedom, in other words, purchased by the elimination of the power of affect in the role of activity. Once this pseudo-freedom is accorded the status of a ground—as it first did in the thought of Descartes—the order of things has been turned on its head.

The real problem is therefore this: how can the human being constitute the origin of its own desires, tense up his own bowstring, as it were? "Even before the eye aims at something to make its conquest," Kierkegaard writes, "it is necessary to capture the eye so that it may belong to him and not he to the eye."[11] The eye, the fundamental intentionality of consciousness in reaching out to the world, must first capture itself, ground itself upon itself, transcendentally dislocate itself from its drives—this is the only way to preserve its autonomy. But there precisely is the rub: is not the *eye seeing itself*, the radical transparency of consciousness to itself, the pseudo-reality par excellence?

As the incipient moment of the experience of nihilation, then, there is the human encounter with the in-principle opacity of its own drives. At first, indeed, this encounter is not confronted in its radical dimension: what resists human intentionality is displaced onto a particular object—I am incapable vis-à-vis some particular drive stimulated by an object. Particular drives, perhaps, can be successfully isolated and overcome through various techniques. One can learn to quit smoking, for example. But concentrating upon particular moments of self-overcoming occludes the more basic problem: it fails to confront the basic structure of human drives, human affectivity, as such. It avoids the ontological problem, which is the problem of whether consciousness has mastery of itself.

This problem cannot be answered decisively within the horizon of human encounters with "external" objects. On this the tradition was perhaps correct: no matter how immense the opposing force, to the extent that it is opposing, it can be faced, objectified, relativized. Human power can persist heroically. But what if what resists the human is unleashed at the center of human reality itself? Then "he struggles not with the world, but with himself."[12] If the affects underlying desire are opaque, this must be understood. The ground of this opacity is nothing other than an involvement of human reality in its own condition, its "internal" relation to itself. The affects originarily arise and are made possible by a strange tie the human has to itself, its being bound to itself: without being two, it nevertheless finds itself opposed to itself. This is the radical fact. To be opposed to and by oneself is to be opposed to and by nothing determinate; consequently, no counter-force can be brought to bear: "Observe him now; his powerful figure is held embraced by another figure; and they hold each other so firmly interlocked and are so equally matched in strength that the wrestling cannot even begin, because in that moment that other figure would overwhelm him—but that other figure is himself."[13] Just what is this deadlock, a deadlock that defines human *incapability*—namely, for self-overcoming? In suffering the deadlock of absolute internal opposition, the human being encounters its own nothingness (and therefore its truth).

Kierkegaard's idea is that it is constitutive of human reality in its primordial dimension to not be able to oppose itself to itself, to get a grip on itself, to exit its own involvement with itself. Rather, the human finds itself given to itself, and given to itself in such a way that cannot be shrugged off. In this absolute inability to absolve itself of the bond with itself lies the radical meaning of human incapability. Concretely this bond is unleashed in the affects that now, understood out of their original source, present themselves as insuperable. So long as the self cannot clear a space of distance and reflection between itself and itself—or so long as there isn't a clearance always already available to it within that which it is, a "world" in which it always already is[14]—freedom as spontaneity will be groundless. And Kierkegaard's language is precise here: the *moment* does not exist wherein the self can get an upper hand, so to speak, on itself—there is no *time* for that. What is needed is time, time as the very breaking of the deadlock, the accomplishment of capability amidst incapability. But time, the instant of what the medievals called the "dilation of the soul," does not have its source in human capability.

The two selves

To elaborate human incapability Kierkegaard constructs a little dialogical encounter between two selves: the "first self" and the "deeper self." The relation between these two selves, however, does not correspond to the relation wherein the self discovers itself opposed to itself. The two selves are distinguished by their differing relation to human incapability. It is a question of what qualifies for each as self-knowledge. The first self is oriented in the direction of discovering and elaborating its own capabilities, its power to economize, adapt, establish its continuity in being. In short, the first self is oriented toward being as a *project* of being, upon the basis of its initiative. It is guided by the ideals of self-transparency, self-determination, perhaps an infinite psycho-analysis.

What is the problem with this first self's self-understanding? Initially—so the "deeper self" responds—it is that the project of establishing one's being on the power to establish oneself in an economy of being fails to take account of the radical contingency of the world, the fact that "even at this moment everything can be changed."[15] There remains an unbreachable schism between self-consciousness and its projects and the gyrations of the world. The first self allowed itself to overlook that; the deeper self, if it knows anything, it knows this: that everything can be undone in an instant. Everything. It "does not give ground or haggle" on this one point.

In fact the logos of the deeper self is very simple and irrefutable: the non-economizable fatality has always already struck, one needn't wait for its appearance—it consists in the fact of being given as such, being handed over to oneself with no exit. No project can work its way out of this deadlock. There is an excess of *need* (*Trængselen*) in principle disproportionate to recuperation through the project: a fundamental lack. As long as the first self understands this, Kierkegaard says, the two selves share a "little secret understanding." The deeper self has nothing opposed to projects as projects; in fact, it endorses the first self's projects. Its opposition arises only when the project structure is allowed to occlude the decisive issue, the fundamental need of the human being.

Self-knowledge: reversal of intentionality

This discourse, like others, again returns to the topos of self-knowledge—since Socrates, at least, a privileged site to reflect on the being of the human being. The question is not about forming an adequate concept of the human being, but realizing its truth. Kierkegaard's guiding thought has been that the human being realizes the truth of its being in its own nihilation, that is, in its encounter with a fundamental incapacity that bears, not upon this or that, but bears on its being itself. Vis-à-vis itself it is capable of nothing, nothing at all. This is the "secret of truth." Yet to encounter this truth, precisely in its intimacy, is no easy work; it is the deepening of self-knowledge. And Kierkegaard thinks the thought to its end: grasping one's own incapability is not something that one is as such capable of. There is an incapability of incapability. He writes: "This is the highest and the most difficult thing of which the human being is capable—yet what am I saying—he is even incapable of this."[16] This wards off any thought of a dialectical movement of truth produced within consciousness' own resources; consciousness cannot produce of itself the genuine encounter with nihilation. It is in particular not capable of "positing itself" as other than itself and then rediscovering therein its richer identity. On the contrary, the incapability of the self consists in the absolute inability to posit itself. Or, in Kierkegaard's formulation, a "human being is not capable of overcoming himself."[17]

Nevertheless, there is a turn in the discourse. The eye that sees and the hand that grasps seem to operate under their own intentionality, through the spontaneity of the I Can. This ecstatic relation to the world, the self finding itself existing in a world already constituted by possibilities addressed to its capability, is annihilated in the encounter with human incapability. The world of possibility coincides with the world wherein the project structure is ultimate; the "deeper self" however has announced the non-ultimacy of the world of project. Human existence is rather structured around a need, a lack, which is in principle oblique to the project. The turn in the discourse consists in reinscribing this lack as precisely a perfection, a power. But in what sense? In the sense that in the anguish of incapability, in its nihilation, the self discovers for the first time the power by which it exists, the very power of being, as not originating in itself, and yet as bearing essentially and intimately on its own self, and therefore as capable of liberating the self from the self. If a self-overcoming is possible it will be on the strength of this power, both intimate and irreducible to the self's ownmost possibility.

Kierkegaard has a ready language to indicate this power of being: "God." "Is it not so, my listener, that these two correspond to each: God and the human being?"[18] In the relation between these two "the human being is great and at his highest when he corresponds to God by being nothing himself at all."[19] Encountering one's own incapability is itself encountering God; it is not a prelude to such an encounter, it *is* the encounter. Thus self-knowledge wholly coincides with a knowledge that "God exists." Kierkegaard insists on this point: any other knowledge of God—whether through a belief assertion or through conceptually founded knowledge—is a mere "pious deception" (*fromt Bedrag*): "Insofar as a person does not know himself in such a way that he himself is capable of nothing at all, he does not actually become conscious in the deeper sense that God exist."[20] It is consequently vain to think or speak or assert that "God exists" outside the phenomenological context in which one grasps one's absolute incapability. Indeed, in terms of this tight correspondence between the human being's encounter with its own nihilation and knowledge of God— so tight that the one *is* the other—the onto-theological problem of God recedes before the problem of self-overcoming, of living out of a wholly new basis.

Self-overcoming is therefore not the self's own movement beyond itself— disclosed as impossible—but rather the overcoming of the structure of the self as such, the self as accessing itself through project, through contact with the most intimate, yet absolutely irreducible, power through which it exists at all. Life on such a basis is difficult, Kierkegaard concedes. For example, it must work itself out in the attunement whereby one is convinced that, on the basis of one's own spontaneity, one is "unable to be happy about the most happy event."[21] The most immediate affects, the burst of joy, transpire in the strength of a power irreducible to the self's ownmost power. The intentionality of the eye that sees and the hand that grasps must be ascribed to a wholly different source. It is a question of inhabiting this attunement whereby the self is, as it were, constantly surprised by itself, "jubilating" in itself.

PART TWO

OCCASIONS OF AFFIRMATION: OCCASIONAL DISCOURSES (1845)

5

The non-place of truth: discourse on confession (1845)[1]

Picasso once said: "I do not seek, I find." If this sounds paradoxical it is because in the Western philosophical tradition finding is somehow always understood as conditioned by, and relative to, a prior seeking. One cannot find without having sought—or, at least, this is taken as true with respect to the "highest" things. Even if one can stumble upon a deposit of gold without having sought it, one generally does not say this about the real, the truth, the absolute. But why not? How is it that the pursuit of truth, the search for it, has come to be regarded as essential to its legitimate acquisition? Whence derives the necessity of the search? This is a question at stake in a discourse Kierkegaard wrote on confession from a little book titled *Three Discourses on Imagined Occasions* (1845). Employing the theological idiom he inherits, the discourse asks: "what does it mean to seek God?" But what is really crucial in this discourse, I'll suggest, is the manner in which Kierkegaard interrogates and finally revaluates the very idea that truth is something that can be sought.

On the way toward clarifying an account of confession, this discourse traces an arc of revaluation in the notion of truth: from truth as the object of a search to truth as what is always already *given*, prior to any search. Kafka, a reader of

Kierkegaard, managed to express this revaluation in his own way: "He who seeks does not find; but he who does not seek will be found."[2] Kierkegaard pursues this revaluation on the occasion of confession. Confession was a very determinate occasion, both theologically and liturgically, in Kierkegaard's Lutheran Denmark.[3] However, Kierkegaard takes confession up as an "imagined occasion" (*tænkte Lejlighed*)—which will mean, not only a "thought up" occasion, but an occasion *for thought*. What is important here is that the occasion of confession consists in the prevailing of a certain "stillness" (*Stilheden*), in a cessation of both speech and activity. To conceive truth in another way than as the object of a seeking is to conceive it as what becomes available only within the context of stillness. Thus Kierkegaard links confession to a movement of becoming still: to confess truth will not mean to bring the truth to light in language, in a speech act, but to become still. Moreover, as I shall explain below, when Kierkegaard speaks of "stillness" he is invoking what he explicitly calls the "infinite nothing" from which it is impossible to separate human existence. The work of confession, we shall see, will involve allowing nothingness "to be."

The metaphysics of the search

Let me begin by considering how it is that seeking seems essential in relation to the truth. The question here is: under what condition does the truth, the absolute, present itself as the object or goal of a search? It is only necessary to *seek* truth on the condition that it is not immediately available in its full presence, or where it is present only under the form of its withdrawal. In other words, seeking the truth is necessary only on condition that the seeker initially lacks truth and understands himself or herself in terms of this lack. However, as Plato and Hegel both knew, the experience of lack is complex: it would seem that the experience of lack is but the obverse side of desire. Thus the search for truth may be understood as a modality of desire. To be in a condition of desire is to be oriented toward some absent plenum. Desire or *eros*, as Diotima said, is the offspring of poverty and plenty: to desire is already be in relation to what would fulfill one, yet without overcoming the lack.[4] If seeking is essential, then, this presupposes an understanding of human existence organized around some missing plenum, some elusive object of desire. Indeed, in the Western tradition, the very notion of philosophy, as the "love of wisdom," has been understood as the *desire* for wisdom. The philosopher is the seeker *par excellence*—which is to say that the philosopher understands the truth of human existence to lie within the search itself. It is the philosopher who understands the centrality of lack and desire in human existence. Moreover, it is no doubt for this reason that, within philosophy, the form of the question is regarded as prior to, more basic than, any answer (e.g. Socrates).

Now confession, in the sense Kierkegaard expresses it, involves neither a search for wisdom nor the experience of an essential lack. Confession is not a modality of desire. His understanding of confession will not, therefore, coincide with the Augustinian account. Augustine's *Confessions*, one could say, involves an effort to inscribe the act of confession, which had a theological meaning, within the context of desire.[5] In confession the "restless heart" seeks that elusive thing that would bring it to rest, fulfill it. It seeks absolute knowledge, which is to say, to align its self-understanding with the divine understanding of it; it seeks to see itself the way the divine sees it, and so bring itself into perfect coincidence with the absolute. And yet this point of identity remains ever out in front of it, never arrived at—the continued object, in other words, of a search. For Kierkegaard, though, the decisive experience is not that of lack or desire, but—we shall see—that of *despair*.

However, this is to get too far ahead; it will be necessary to back up. In this little discourse Kierkegaard expresses a position in which "everything is reversed" (*Alt vendes om*), a position in which this extremely powerful tradition of search is revaluated. To catch sight of this revaluation, therefore, Kierkegaard appropriately starts at the beginning—namely, at what the philosophical tradition of desire identifies as its *own* beginning. Both Plato and Aristotle are in agreement: philosophy begins in *wonder*.[6] So this is where Kierkegaard's discourse on confession begins: by recapitulating the beginning of philosophy in wonder. The revaluation Kierkegaard expresses then takes shape as the effort to show how this "first beginning" in wonder has already exhausted itself and opened the possibility of a "second beginning," what he calls "the true beginning." As we shall see, confession, as a relation to truth, only has significance in relation to this second beginning.

The first beginning: wonder

Kierkegaard's discourse deals with "what it means to seek God"—it is a discourse, then, which takes up what it means to seek. Initially, this takes place as the effort to clarify the origin of seeking. It asks: out of what exigence does seeking arise? Kierkegaard's answer, referring to the account of the beginning of philosophy found in Plato and Aristotle, which he summarily calls "pagan" thought, is that seeking begins out of the affectivity of wonder (*Forundringen*). Wonder constitutes the affective condition in which seeking arises. So what is wonder? According to Kierkegaard wonder is an "ambiguous condition of the soul,"[7] characterized by "fear and blessedness"; it is the condition in which the human being is gripped by the enigmatic character of being, an experience close to what Rudolph Otto called the "experience of the Holy." In wonder the enigmatic fact that there is anything at all, the enigma of being itself, the enigma of the origin, resonates. But in the affective condition of wonder the origin appears as precisely "the unknown" (*det Ubekjendte*). Thus wonder is the attunement in which the withdrawn and unknown origin presents itself within human life, awakening it to the search. Wonder constitutes in itself a beginning, the "beginning of all deeper understanding."[8]

In his discourse Kierkegaard gives an account of how this attunement finds diverse expressions in human life. Without considering all of these permutations, one can underline as of particular importance that for Kierkegaard wonder gives rise to efforts to *grasp the origin conceptually*, to come to know what is unknown. At first, wonder finds expression in various forms of "superstition" (*Overtroen*) whose concepts are childish and unwieldy. Nevertheless the overall trajectory of wonder—at least under the guiding hand of the Greeks—was to grasp the real, the origin, under the concept of a "highest good." According to Kierkegaard this is the premier Greek concept, the Greek word for the real. Greek thought cleans up the superstition and organizes human existence around the concept of a highest good which, precisely as highest, remains indeterminate and indeed unknown. It is in relation to this "highest good," as the unknown, that the wish (or desire) arises: "the other goods have names ... but where the wish draws its deepest breath, where this unknown seems to manifest itself, there is wonder."[9]

The attunement of wonder around a "highest good," which is "not defined by its relation to other goods, precisely because it is highest," also receives the name "God."[10] Thus, in the Greek context—a context which, as Kierkegaard explains, "is experienced again in each generation"—the object of wonder is doubly-named: the highest good and God. One could say wonder is oriented around the highest good as God, or God as the highest good. In each case what is at stake is an ultimate principle (*archē*), which precisely as ultimate, remains undetermined. One could perhaps here invoke the concept of an ontotheological foundation: namely, the conflation of being with *a highest being*. In these terms, the "Greek" understanding of the origin translates easily into a theological context and, therefore, one may not only speak of wonder, but also of "worship" (*Tilbedelsen*) as an attunement that belongs to wonder.

The essential thing about wonder, however, is that it arouses desire—"the wish" and "striving"—and thus gives rise to seeking. Wonder—being-gripped by being as indeterminate—casts human life into an essential search for a *determinate expression* of the origin. Yet at the same time wonder keeps the seeker in salutary suspense. In wonder the essential truth seems always just about to manifest itself, yet never does; truth remains under withdrawal. Thus wonder involves a conception of truth as something transcendent. Nevertheless, according to Kierkegaard, the overall orientation of wonder, inasmuch as it seeks a concept of the origin, is toward *knowledge*. Wonder wants to know the origin, conceptually to grasp it, to articulate it—or, if nothing else, to express why it cannot be expressed. Wonder, in short, is finally a theoretical attitude; it wants to *see*. "Often deluded," Kierkegaard writes, "wonder wants *to see where it is going* and no longer walk in the dark."[11] Wonder thus gives rise to *theoria* in the same moment it gives rise to desire. Hence these three terms—wonder, desire, *theoria*—constitute the core terms of the "Greek" beginning.

As already indicated, however, Kierkegaard understands wonder as the "first beginning" and not the "true beginning." This will indicate that at stake in the "second beginning" is something other than the inception of *theoria*. It will indicate that knowledge is not the privileged domain in which the relation to truth transpires. And finally, it will indicate that seeking, something conditioned by wonder, is not the ultimate modality of the relation to truth. But in order to see this it is necessary to clarify how the first beginning encounters its own limit, how it gives way to another beginning.

The epoch/epoché of wonder

Kierkegaard's discourse is written from what might be called a historical premise: namely, that "wonder was gone; it is gone." He writes: "There was a time in the world when humankind, weary of wonder, weary of fate, turned away from the external and discovered that there was no object of wonder, that the unknown was nothing and the wonder was a deception."[12] Thus Kierkegaard's discourse is marked by the sense that something decisive has happened: wonder has grown stale, the epoch of wonder has exhausted itself. The Greek beginning is at its end. We are weary of wonder. This is a weariness that hangs over, for example, the entirety of Hegel's thought, finding expression in his comment that philosophy should give up the love of wisdom—i.e. the incessant search for it—in order to become wisdom itself.[13] Kierkegaard explains this weariness in terms of the extraordinary growth of knowledge. If wonder is already implicitly oriented toward *theoria*, it consumes itself, or sublates itself, when this becomes explicitly developed in knowledge.

However, it is a very specific conception of knowledge that has supplanted wonder: knowledge that is certain of itself, that possesses its own presuppositions. Kierkegaard writes: "If the seeker is presumed to be able to do everything to find what is sought ... there is nothing to wonder over."[14] By invoking the presumption of capability, Kierkegaard references the sort of knowledge operative in modern culture—namely, *methodically acquired knowledge*. Modernity is the time in which wonder is exhausted insofar as modern culture is organized, no longer around seeking, but more precisely around *method*; and method, understood within modernity, is a way of proceeding that can be certain of itself.

As clarified in Descartes' various meditations, certainty has a very precise locus: it can be found only within the ego's relation to itself. Only that which can present itself within the milieu of self-certainty may be considered real. To this extent, self-consciousness offers itself—to Descartes and to modern culture—as a new foundation. Now, this is the exact point where wonder is displaced. In the context of a methodical pursuit of truth, knowledge no longer takes one beyond the orbit of self-consciousness. The ecstatic relation to being in wonder is cut off at its root. Kant formulated the ontological milieu of immanence as the very structure of knowledge in the following sentence: "The a priori conditions for a possible experience as such are at the same time conditions for the possibility of objects of experience."[15] Knowing transpires within the ontological milieu of immanence. In these terms, there is everything to explain, but nothing to wonder over;[16] everything to manipulate, nothing to desire. The seeker, presumed to be able to find what is sought, is always assured in advance of victory. Thus, in the growth of self-assured knowledge, we are to see the self-consummation or self-exhausting of wonder, namely of the "first beginning."

Despair and the revaluation of truth

It is at this moment, where self-consciousness offers itself as a new foundation and the search cedes place to method, that another beginning becomes possible. Indeed, here it is possible, Kierkegaard thinks, to catch sight of the "true wonder." Yet this is a moment of intense ambiguity, simultaneously of closure and opening, of ending and beginning. It is the moment of revaluation, of passage from one conception of truth to another: from truth as the object of desire held anticipatively in view, to truth as what is given prior to desire. Now according to Kierkegaard the passage from one conception of truth to another is mediated by a very definite phenomenon—that of despair. Despair, he says, is the *Tankestreg*,[17] the dash, simultaneously the hiatus between the two beginnings and what connects them. When wonder exhausts itself, human reality loses its ecstatic openness to being, its desire. It suffers the experience of being unable to exit itself. This is the experience of despair. Despair, Kierkegaard says, is the sense of being "trapped in existence, trapped forever."[18] Despair is decisive here, even capable of inaugurating something new, insofar as it puts the self into contact with its own givenness and, thereby, with *givenness as such*. Despair is really the polar opposite of wonder: whereas wonder involves the ecstatic opening to the outside, despair is the self's implosion into itself.

Despair is the anti-erotic mood *par excellence*. An existence filled with despair is the opposite of an existence tensed up with desire. In despair the self finds itself riveted to itself and thus deprived of any ecstatic opening. Thus, in despair, seeking loses any basis or motive. Far from propelling one into a search for the truth, despair only propels one into a *flight*—namely the effort to flee oneself. In a strikingly Augustinian phrase, Kierkegaard writes "where then does one flee in order to escape oneself?"[19] The answer is "nowhere"; flight from self is impossible and this is indeed the very experience of despair. Though seeking and fleeing may be mistaken for each other—they both involve movement—in reality they are completely contrary. Fleeing, unlike seeking, is not conditioned by desire, nor by the sense of lack; rather, it is conditioned by something all too close, all too pressing.

If despair renders seeking impossible, however, this very impossibility can serve as the point where, as Kierkegaard says, "everything is reversed." In despair the truth presents itself under an entirely new aspect: it is not what human reality essentially lacks, it is not the ever-withdrawn object of desire, but that which is always already *given*. Inasmuch as it involves the self's impossibility to escape itself, despair is the self's encounter, for the first time, with its own insuperable givenness. Moreover, it is this very givenness, precisely as something unsurpassable, which is now taken as the essential quality of truth. If there is something inaugural or epoch-opening in despair, then, it is that it reveals givenness, or more precisely self-givenness, as the milieu of truth. Kierkegaard articulates the reversal at stake in the following passage: "If that which is sought for is assumed to be given, [then] seeking means that the one seeking is himself changed, *so that he becomes the place where that which is sought can be in truth.*"[20] Rather than seeking the truth—which in any event is impossible inasmuch as the truth is already given—the seeker is to become the very site where truth can occur. The seeker is to become the site where the truth can be true, where it can be.

The whole problem of seeking the truth is thus transformed: it is no longer a question of striving to bring oneself closer to a truth that is remote, that belongs to a "there" to be distinguished from a "here" in a distance that cannot be crossed. Such seeking of the truth always operates within a prior directedness, a certain pre-understanding of the "where" of truth. But the givenness of truth indicated in despair signifies that it has arrived prior to the formation of a pre-understanding that could receive it. Truth arrives in an unbidden way; unbiddenness is the very quality of truth. What is unbidden is undergone, what one cannot not undergo, and what is undergone in this way is the not at all the same as what is desired. In short, what Kierkegaard articulates here is an anti-erotics of truth. Truth has always already *struck*, as it were, prior to any desire for it, and so it is a question Kierkegaard says of "going backwards," of becoming what one already is, the site of an arrival. Now, as I shall say more about in a moment, to become the place where truth can be true is the work of confession.

First, however, I want to linger a bit on this new understanding of truth. According to the "Greek" conception of truth Kierkegaard begins with, the truth presents itself as a "highest" instance, a remote object. The true or absolute, precisely as highest, remains unknowable. Nevertheless, within this Greek conception the truth is still what calls for knowledge, what awakens the desire for knowledge. Thus on this conception the knower is not himself or herself the very site of truth, but must rather move toward truth, from one site to another site. On this conception the absolute is always and essentially "elsewhere." The knower is alienated from the true. However, within the reversal Kierkegaard articulates, the truth is not elsewhere but precisely "here." It is already given. Yet its mode of being given is not given-as-an-object, not even as a withdrawn object. The truth is given as the subject's givenness to itself, namely within the experience of despair. Thus one can see the reversal at issue: truth, the absolute, can never receive the shape of objectivity. This can be contrasted, for example, with the basic intuition of Hegel's that the absolute has necessary recourse to objectivity as a moment in its coming to the awareness of itself. For Kierkegaard, the form of objectivity itself, which is always geared to the interests of knowledge, is incompatible with truth. Hence truth, as given, cannot be known. The truth here is too close to be known, too present. To know the truth, or to seek the truth, presupposes a minimal distance between knower and known. However, where the self is itself the site of truth, the place where truth can be true, there is no distance between the self and truth—and *so* it cannot be known. One can only *be* truth, one can never know it.

For this reason, Kierkegaard says, "one can know everything and not have made a beginning with the least thing." The act of knowing, oriented toward something external and not given, occludes the givenness of truth, i.e. the knower as the *site* of truth. "All knowledge," Kierkegaard adds, "is only a presupposition" (*kun en Forudsætning*). To claim, as he has, that knowledge has the inner structure of a presupposing is to allude to the problem of positing (*setzen*) in German idealism. It says that knowing always posits (*sætte*) something prior (*forud*) to itself as its inner condition. It does not posit, to be exact, any particular content; rather, as Fichte showed in his *Science of Knowledge*, the subject posits *itself* as the condition for knowledge. Yet truth, in its quality of givenness, arrives prior to the self which posits itself, prior therefore to the formation of a horizon of pre-understanding. It cannot be properly received and contextualized by a subject, it can only be undergone. It cannot be set forth in front of one as an object; it is always behind one. Again, all one can do with truth is to become the place where truth can *be* true.

Additionally, the always prior givenness of truth leads to a curious paradox: the very givenness of truth makes it initially unavailable—or, if one likes, ungiven. Truth does not reside in a "there" to be distinguished from a "here." Inasmuch as it is neither "here" nor "there," truth is nowhere. But it is nowhere simply by the fact that it is absolutely here—which is to say, belongs to a "here" that cannot be opposed to any "there." One thus encounters again the strange paradox that the seeker could lose the truth precisely by trying to find it. To launch upon a quest for that which is nowhere is just to lose one's way. The only thing one can do, Kierkegaard says, is to turn from the forward movement of seeking and go "backwards." One is always already past the truth, ecstatically past it, seeking it elsewhere, precisely because it is too close to be seen. Thus the initial orientation of the person is not in any way neutral, but rather is a modality of losing a relation to truth. Losing access to the truth is the initial and normal mode of relating to it. One has to do nothing other than "stand there" and lose a relation to the "here" in which truth is given. To catch sight of this paradox, a paradox that stands at the inception of the "true beginning," is enough to awaken the wonder of the entire human being: "But that what is sought is given, that it is possessed by the person who in misunderstanding stands there and is losing it—that awakens the wonder of the whole person"[21] (403/23). The "true wonder" is thus the perplexity of coming to grips with the event of truth—that it has always already struck prior to the subject's having made itself ready for it. This wonder does not give rise to seeking, but rather to what Kierkegaard will call confession.

Confession

So now we come finally to confession. As one may have gathered, confession is not so much the theme of Kierkegaard's discourse as the *occasion* for the discourse. Beginning at the beginning of philosophy—namely, with wonder—the discourse has elaborated a revaluation in the conception of truth: truth is not something to be sought, it is not the object of desire, but rather that which arrives always prior to being sought. Truth has always already found the seeker. To seek truth or embark upon a quest for truth is therefore already to abandon the site where truth can *be* true. The very search for truth is the fundamental errancy of the human being. But then, we may ask, what is one to do in relation to truth, if one cannot seek it? Indeed, Kierkegaard asks himself in mid-discourse: "Is there nothing at all to do, then?"[22] In a certain sense, there is nothing to do. In relation to truth what is essential is the cessation of doing, or "becoming still."

Confession is often understood as a work of language. In Augustine, for example, confession takes the form of a narration. The confessing self constitutes itself as a truthful self by confessing. By narrating its own errancy, it seeks to bring into being a self-understanding that comes closer to the divine understanding of it. Its own narration thereby brings truth into being, it "makes true" (*facere veritatem*) the divine truth. And for Augustine the narration itself is an expression of desire: through narration the self seeks a truth that remains transcendent, held in the divine gaze. In the terms Kierkegaard's discourse sketches, however, Augustine can be said to have reinscribed the act of confession into the first beginning, the Greek beginning. He retains wonder (Augustine would call it worship) and desire as the inceptive affects. The reason why Kierkegaard's discourse on confession has had recourse to what looks like a detour—namely, to the distinction between a first beginning and a second, true beginning—is that he found it necessary to detach confession from any idea that something gets *constituted* in confession. Confession is exactly not about *making* the truth, it is about becoming the site where truth can of itself occur. It is therefore not a work of language. Confession is an undoing, a deconstituting, a going backward. The relation between confession and the "infinite nothing" is essential.

This is important to underline because, as he elaborates his understanding of confession as a concrete movement late in the discourse, Kierkegaard returns to themes that seem familiar: confession, which is always "before God," is about confessing *sin*, repenting, becoming transparent (*gjennemsigtig*), achieving forthrightness or honesty (*Oprigtigheden*) in regard to oneself. All of these motifs, which are thoroughly classical, would be deeply misunderstood outside of the context of revaluation in which Kierkegaard inserts them— namely in the context of stillness. Stillness, which involves the quieting of speech and activity, is the phenomenological site in which the "infinite nothing" can show itself. Now, as Kierkegaard says, "one cannot give oneself this stillness."[23] To seek stillness, to undertake the *project* of becoming still, is already to lose a relation to it. Therefore to become still is not to undertake a project; it is not an action structured around an end-goal. And yet becoming still is not a simple absence of doing either. Becoming still is neither a doing nor a non-doing. So if confession involves, for example, the confession of "sin," such a non-acting act will necessarily receive a different sense than the usual one—namely, the bringing to light of something in language.

In fact Kierkegaard very carefully formulates what confession of sin would mean. The movement of confession has, of course, a very determinate meaning within the theological tradition Kierkegaard inherits as the basis of this discourse. In particular, confession has an essential relation to the theological-dogmatic category of "sin" and, via this concept, refers to notions of purity and guilt. Kierkegaard cites the biblical text: "*no one without purity can see God, and sin is impurity, and therefore no one can see God without becoming a sinner.*"[24] Understood as a movement, therefore, confessing is identical to "becoming a sinner." What will be decisive here, however, is the nature of this becoming. What is it, not to *be* a sinner, but to *become* a sinner? And how is one to understand the category of "sin" within the phenomenological context the discourse has already elaborated? Kierkegaard makes it explicit that to confess is neither to confess anything particular, it is not a "counting of all particular sins," nor is it to confess some universal condition of the human. "A confessor," says Kierkegaard, "is not a co-signatory in the human race's enormous account book."[25]

Neither particular nor universal, sin is the category of the *singular and determinate* (*den enkelte og bestemte*). The reality of sin cannot be grasped through the logic of a general norm in relation to particular acts. What breaks open this logic, demanding the category of singularity, is that sin "has continuity internal to itself" (*Sammenhæng i sig selv*). The concept of immanent continuity is essential here. Sin signifies, namely, that power by which singular acts do not simply fall punctually within time—and therefore fall off by themselves as particulars—but rather become productive of other acts. Sin signifies, in other words, the category by which Kierkegaard grasps human existence in its durational or continuous temporality. But of this continuity Kierkegaard writes that it is necessary to understand "that from the singular sin and going astray there is a continuity, an unfathomable continuity." Sin is thus the determination of existence as marked by continuities that escape it, that are unfathomable to it; or, more precisely, it signifies the manner in which the self identifies itself with its projects. It thereby inverts the problem of transparency: it substitutes its self-reflective awareness of itself for its real life.[26] Yet this difference cannot become apparent to it except on condition of becoming still. If one likes, one could say the self only realizes it has an unconscious in becoming still. The "infinite nothing" marks itself as an opacity at the heart of the self and "sin" is the name for the occlusion of this opacity.[27]

Conclusion

As the reader reads this discourse, working through the "first beginning" in wonder to its self-sublation in knowledge, working across the phenomenology of despair to a new understanding of truth as given, the reader could well ask him or herself: how is this discourse on confession? It is certainly a strange discourse that links confessing, not to a speech-act, but to becoming still. However, this is where the title may offer some help: the discourse is about the *occasion* of confession as much as confession itself. In a concrete way, confession demands stillness. But what Kierkegaard has done is to take this concrete occasion and raised it to the level of an ontological problematic: it is not simply about, for example, the silence of a church or confession booth—it is not liturgical silence—but about a stillness that permeates human reality. This stillness is neither here nor there; it has no determinate site. It is nowhere (or everywhere).

To become aware of stillness is to become aware, at the same time, of the way in which one's life is concretely predicated upon the occlusion of stillness. Concretely human life is always already involved in project and in the anticipative aiming at end-goals. Givenness appears only as that point *from which* possibilities are projected. What does not appear concretely is that immemorial instant in which the self is given and given to itself. So to confess is indeed to go backwards, to return to a still origin, the nothing, prior to the birth of desire, prior to the irruption of the project. This is the dimension of human reality, the dimension of its truth, which is neither constituted nor constitutable.

6

On being-together-with-death: discourse "At a Graveside" (1845)

At a Graveside is unique among Kierkegaard's discourses in that, though allusions to biblical texts abound, the discourse itself does not take shape as a commentary on any specific biblical text. Moreover the discourse invokes no specific theological or dogmatic interpretation of death. Not one word is said, for example, of an "afterlife." Indeed, the discourse systematically disavows, as mere representations, the usual efforts to grasp death as meaningful: death as sleep, as relief from hardship, as great equalizer, as the transition to another life, as the "wages of sin," as a "great transformation." All of these conceptions, which are both theological and popular, are dismissed as evasions; none of them *think* death. And that is the sole task offered by this discourse: "to think oneself together with death" (*tænker sig selv sammen med Døden*).

The discourse is thus organized around the distinction between thinking death and merely representing it. The opposite of thinking death is to let oneself experience it through the mediation of a *mood*: "To think oneself dead is seriousness; to be witness to the death of another is mood."[1] Moods constitute the milieu of representations. Moods effect a radical displacement of death, turning death into an event that can be observed *from the outside*, and consequently letting death be encountered only through distancing—namely, through the mediation of a representation, a symbol or universal notion.

To think oneself together with death is to relate to death without any mediation or distance. It is to forego all interpretation of death, to withdraw death from any context of meaning. Death *means* nothing. And not only this: death does not ground or open meaning. In the expression "to think oneself together with death" the essential word is "together with" (*sammen med*): death can in no way be integrated into life, it is rather life's absolute other; and yet it is essential to draw death into *proximity* with life, to place them side by side, as it were, without mediation. In thinking death without mediation rather than on the basis of a mood, Kierkegaard says, death acquires a "retroactive power" (*Tilbagevirkende Kraft*) capable of "reshaping life" (*omdanner Livet*). It will be of the highest importance, however, to consider how death may affect this transformation in life. It will neither be a question of "tarrying with the negative" (Hegel) nor assuming an "existential project" of being-toward-death (Heidegger). The discourse refuses what both Hegel and Heidegger grant: the conception of death ("the negative") as the radical origin of meaning, the very opening of human existence to its possibilities, the very foundation of all of its projects. For Kierkegaard, death cannot be integrated into life; and yet, at the same time, the evasion of the reality of death is the evasion of existence *par excellence*. Death must be confronted in its reality without making it the touchstone of truth. If life gains meaning it can only be through life itself.

Thinking death/death's decision

Thinking oneself together with death, drawing it into proximity with life, coincides with "becoming serious." Seriousness (*Alvor*) is a modality of human existence that arises only in thinking death: "The seriousness is that it is death that you are thinking; and that you are thinking it as your lot. You thereby do what death is not capable of doing: that you are and that death also is."[2] Kierkegaard's discourse here makes obvious and critical reference to Epicurus' famous dictum: "when we are, death is not; and when death is, we are not."[3] This is to effect a caesura between death and existence: death cannot in principle be made present; death is therefore "nothing to us," we whose very existence is constituted as presence. Death and life can in no wise be conjoined or integrated. They do not even oppose each other; rather, they simply exclude one another. Life in itself has no relation with death just as death in itself has no relation with life. Another way to put this is: death is the non-representable *par excellence*. But for Epicurus this means: death should *not* be taken seriously. Owing to its simple falling-outside-of-life, death has no relevance for life whatsoever.

Kierkegaard's discourse assumes, as in principle possible, what Epicurus denies: that death can be made present to life—thought—without transmuting it into the pseudo-reality of representation. Death *can* be thought, that is, made proximate to life, without thereby losing its essence. Such thinking, as will be seen, does not involve the positive elaboration of the content of death—and in this sense Kierkegaard, just as much as Epicurus, denounces all representations of death. To think death is rather to clarify the modalities of a non-meaning that, precisely as such, impinges on human life absolutely. The thought of death does not integrate death into life; it places human existence before this non-meaning, prohibiting its evasion. Death is indeed nothing, but it cannot be heroically conjured away as "nothing for us." Human life gains "seriousness"[4]— that is, finally realizes that something is at stake for it—in facing up to death.

To think death, rather than to interpret it or represent it, is to bring to mind what Kierkegaard calls "death's decision" (*Dødens Afgjørelsen*). The latter phrase must be taken in two senses: on the one hand the reality of death signifies that the fundamental character of human life has always already been decided upon; to exist is, from the beginning, always to exist in terms of this decision. On the other hand, this decision itself—as something constitutive of the condition of the human—must itself be decided upon as an explicit act taken up by the living being. Death decides about me and I decide about death. Kierkegaard elaborates the inner content of death's decision in a threefold manner: death's decision is 1) decisive, 2) indeterminate and 3) inexplicable. Thinking death is thus to make oneself proximate to that which is irreducibly decisive, indeterminate and inexplicable—it is the realization that *there is* something that cannot be made meaningful. This in itself reshapes life.

Death as decisive

Firstly, then, to think death means grasping what is decisive in death's decision. Kierkegaard writes: "On death's decision it must first be said that it is *decisive*. The repetition of the word is the indicative thing."[5] As always, with a repetition, it is a matter of coming to understand oneself through a prior condition that always already precedes and determines the totality of one's existence—in this case, the event that has absolutely decided one's existence. Death is first of all grasped as the irrevocable condition, without appeal, of the human. One could call it the originary judgment at the ground of the human: the human being has been "declared to be" mortal. Thinking the decided characteristic of its being as mortal does not mean, however, treating mortality as an objective fact about the human. Rather, it signifies coming to terms with an absolute breaking-off: with the reality that, in death, "it is over" (*det er forbi*).

In relation to death's decisiveness, however, a mode of evasion emerges that Kierkegaard calls "deferral" *Opsættelse*). It is the task of thinking to dispel this. Deferral occurs where, facing the absolute cut of death, the imagination instead projects a future ahead of itself, thereby occluding death's decisiveness. Deferral becomes a strategy whereby the person understands himself in terms of something fundamentally unreal: the "not yet" of the projected future, in which everything is *not* over. Meaning is once again salvaged, albeit by displacing death's decision. Deferral likewise generates various "ameliorating representations" by which life is imagined beyond the end: for example, in the idea of death as "sleep" or "release from captivity." This projection of oneself into a future happens even among those at the very threshold of death itself: "For in the moment of death itself it can seem to the dying one himself that there is still time." That there will always be time—and consequently that there will always be a way out—constitutes the evasion of death's decisiveness *par excellence*. At some time there will be no time.

The absolutely interruptive quality of death entails a strongly counterintuitive concept. Death is an event, but an event *sui generis*: it is an event that, strictly speaking, happens to no one. That is to say, it is an event that cannot be thought as an experience of a persisting subject. Sickness, for example, is an event in which the self undergoes something, is "tightened in a snare." But when death tightens its snare, Kierkegaard says, "it has indeed caught nothing, because then all is over."[6] Death closes in on precisely no one; when it comes, there is no longer any "I" to close in on. If it is an "event," then, it is but an instant of pure annihilation. Death loses the very thing it captures by capturing it. In all strictness, then, *no one undergoes death* because death is the undoing of all structures of undergoing. To take death's decision decisively is thus to think oneself in relation to an instant of pure annihilation—so pure it cannot be called an annihilation *of* anything. No one is present at his own death; it is not something undergone or experienced. The most immediate consequence of this is that death cannot be conceived as a transition to anything—there would be no one to transition! Death decisiveness will in this way throw life back against itself, with no recourse.

Death as indeterminate

Secondly, to think death's decision also involves thinking oneself in relation to what is absolutely indeterminable (*ubestemmelig*).[7] Seriousness consists in thinking the indeterminable as the indeterminable, namely as pure enigma, as not resolvable into any general conception. At issue here are attempts at constructing a universal notion of death, grasping death in its significance for a general conception of the human condition. To determine death in this way gives rise to two apparently opposing concepts: firstly, death as the "great equalizer" in human life, the very commonness of the common human condition, the most universal event; or, secondly, death as the very expression of particularity, the always contingent event that strikes whom it strikes, without reason and without warning. While these are apparently opposing conceptions, they nevertheless follow from the same logic of inscribing death within a meaningful conceptuality—of determining the meaning of death.

Both of these efforts, however, depend upon a logic of comparison: of grasping things as like one another, which gives rise to the concept of death as the most common of events, or unlike one another, which gives rise to the concept of death as irreducibly particular. The problem with this is that in death nothing is either alike or unlike since death is pure annihilation: nothing is neither like nor unlike nothing. Each interpretation depends upon positing some comparable being that would persist within death and thus not taking the nihilation seriously.

Actually, to interpret death in universal terms as the "great equalizer," Kierkegaard suggests, is to approach it via the mediation of a mood—in this case, the leveling mood of resentment. The weak can tell themselves, for example, that everyone is equal in death and that *therefore* differences in power do not matter. Similarly, concentrating upon the particularity of death is ultimately rooted in multifarious moods, from exuberance to melancholy, united in an interpretation of the human condition as awash in tragic finitude. Once again, rather than indulge mood's interpretation of death, what is necessary is to think death. To think death signifies becoming determinate about the indeterminable: seriousness about death "can determine it." This entails formulating a concept of the indeterminate. Of this Kierkegaard writes:

"Thus death is indeterminable: the only thing certain and the only thing about which nothing certain is known."[8]

Death is on the one hand certain; the "axe already lies at the root of the tree." Human reality has always already been placed under the decision of death. There is no evading this irrevocable decision. Death is, however, essentially uncertain inasmuch as each moment harbors the possibility of death. "The uncertainty," Kierkegaard writes, "is the brief statement: It is possible."[9] Death is not a possibility lying in the future, but a possibility of each present. The uncertainty of death refers less to its "when" and "how," but rather to its incalculable power to render the meaning of the present uncertain: what is the meaning of what I am *now doing* if it can, in an instant, suffer an absolute interruption? Normally the meaning of the present is grounded in an anticipatory relation to the future: the present *will have meant* something from the standpoint of future moment of completion. The activity of ship-building, for example, will have meant something only when there is a completed ship; in itself the activity does not yet mean anything. Death, however, is the in principle possibility of interruption informing every present. Death thereby detaches each present moment from the horizon in which it could acquire meaning—the horizon of the project. Thus, in relation to death's decision human existence cannot establish a properly anticipatory relation with its end; the present moment is detached, in principle, from total meaning. It is cut away in uncertainty about what it will have meant.

In this way thinking death as essentially indeterminate—as certain/uncertain—expresses itself as a praxis of watchfulness: "the certainty of death determines the learner once for all in seriousness, but the uncertainty of death is the daily... necessary watchfulness that watches over the seriousness."[10] The uncertainty, the sense that each moment harbors the possibility of its absolute interruption, fuels attention to "the use of time and the nature of the work"— that is, to whether the work has been undertaken apart from any horizon of fulfillment. Only that work which is entirely valid *in its inception*, entirely independent of whether or not it is brought to completion, is an "essential work" because such work has already taken account of the absolute interruption of death. Death makes it so that time is essentially incomplete; "seriousness" becomes the vessel harboring the energies of inception, of labor justified entirely through itself—justified in its incompletion.

Death as inexplicable

There is a final modality of taking Death's decision seriously in thought: grasping death as "inexplicable" (*uforklarlig*) and allowing it to remain without explication by dogmatic, symbolical or representational content: "Even if human beings find an explanation, death itself explains nothing."[11] In terms of the human effort to explain death, "innumerable evasions are possible." Kierkegaard draws up a shortlist from both ancient and biblical sources: "death as transition, transformation, suffering, a struggle, the last struggle, punishment, the wages of sin."[12] Explanation has a precise function in the economy of evasion: it allows the explainer "to protect himself from the influence of death by means of a mood, which holds death within an equilibrium of undecidedness."[13] As a matter of structure, the very act of explaining death sets it at a distance and thus effaces its reality as permeating existence with decision. Explanation places death on the outside, on a horizon of visibility, and so makes it a matter of *viewing* death. To think of death as inexplicable thus constitutes a refusal to substitute an event of termination, in which meaning can be settled and retroactively gathered up before a gaze, for *the termination of events* as such, in which meaning is disrupted. Thus no theology of death, nor even a philosophy of death, in whatever high or low sense, is possible in thinking death. To think death truly means to bracket out all content by which it may be incorporated in a meaningful structure. With death, "the meaning is banished" (*Meningen er ude*). Death is an exteriority to meaning. The fundamental temptation of the human being is to make death mean something, to regard death as an enigma that needs to be solved. Against this death says: "I need no explanation, but bear in mind that in [death's] decision it is finished and that this can, at any moment, be at hand."[14] Thinking death is the most abstemious, restrictive thought: it is to think *only* the absolute interruptibility of each instant; it is to forego the satisfactions of a theory of death.

Through its triple determination—as decisive, indeterminate and inexplicable—human existence falls, from its very inception, under these determinations. The essential traits of death's decision, in other words, constitute the essential traits of human existence. Thus thinking death *is* thinking existence according to its essential modalities. As a way of gaining analytical clarity about this, it will be useful to compare Kierkegaard's discourse to its contemporary shadow: namely, Heidegger's celebrated analysis of being-toward-death. There is little doubt that Heidegger's analysis owes an essential debt to Kierkegaard's discourse.[15] Indeed, this indebtedness, along with the systematic power of Heidegger's analysis, has led to a certain fusion of their discourses. It is essential, however, to disentangle the two analyses of death. Heidegger's being-toward-death does not coincide with Kierkegaard's thinking of death.

Heidegger's existential project of a being-toward-death

The question that arises in relation to Heidegger's reinscription of Kierkegaard's discourse on death can be stated simply: can Kierkegaard's thinking of death, in particular the manner in which death acquires retroactive power to transform life, be summarized as an "existential project" of death? Is death ultimately to be understood, as in Heidegger, not only as the foundation of the entire project structure but as *itself* a project? The question at stake here concerns the supposed productive power of death, that is, of negation. Is it death that opens human existence—as Heidegger would say—to its "wholeness," that is, to the genuineness of its truth? Does death, when taken as death, carry back human existence to the very source from which meaning arises and so genuinely found human projects?

Heidegger's effort to grasp death in its properly phenomenological meaning, as a "pure phenomena of Dasein,"[16] is systematically motivated by his effort to understand Dasein in terms of the being of Dasein itself. The way of being of Dasein, in its penultimate formulation, he calls "care." Care means, more precisely, "Dasein's being ahead of itself in its always already being involved in something."[17] As care, "Dasein is essentially underway towards something; in caring it is toward itself in that which it is still not."[18] Care indicates that what constitutes the being of Dasein is its "being at issue for itself," its in principle open-endedness in relation to itself, and thus its impossibility of ever being "whole," that is, complete. Dasein never *is*; it is always on the way toward its being: "this points to an impossibility in principle to find oneself in the wholeness of Dasein."[19]

It is at this point that the phenomenon of death intervenes and comes to play a "remarkable" role in Heidegger's discourse. On the one hand, death negates Dasein by reducing it to the status of a finite thing: death signifies that nothing is any longer outstanding for Dasein; it is finished. And "being finished, when asserted about Dasein, means no longer being."[20] This would seem to indicate that death is precisely a power that interrupts Dasein's determination toward wholeness, a power that shatters the guiding anticipation, constitutive of Dasein's existence itself, of being whole. But the remarkable turn in Heidegger's discourse is just this: death is not just an event negating Dasein as Dasein, but a phenomenon over against which Dasein can understand itself in an anticipatory way. Dasein does not merely undergo death, but is able to relate to death through the very structure of care—namely, as an eminent *possibility* still outstanding for it, and consequently something through which it can understand itself. In an anticipatory way Dasein can understand the totality of it being in terms of death and so can make of death precisely the totalizing horizon of its *projects*.

When death is allowed to appear as mediated through the prior structure of care—when it is encountered as a *phenomenon* characterized by its ever-impending possibility—its very meaning is radically altered: "Because Dasein means 'being-ahead-of-itself as care,' it can of itself be its being wholly in every moment of its being."[21] The relation "being-ahead-of-itself as care," properly clarified, is nothing other than the relation of Dasein to its own death: "Care is being-toward-death."[22] Rather than constituting the in-principle impossibility of Dasein experiencing its wholeness, death itself offers the very foundation of wholeness: "insofar as Dasein qua being possible is essentially already its death, it is as Dasein always already a whole."[23] Death is the very power by which Dasein gains access to its own total character, namely, to the total nature of its involvement in the *world* in which it always already finds itself. Death of itself places Dasein within a possible wholeness inasmuch as it: 1) brings up Dasein before *itself*, that is, before its "ownmost" possibility, its very being as being-possible. Thus death grants Dasein to itself as something to "take up." And, 2) understood properly, in terms of its being, death is the very power by which possibility as such is opened, the opening of which constitutes the total horizon in which Dasein can take up any possibility. Death grants possibility as such to Dasein because its very character is being-irreducibly-possible. Being in face of death is identical to being in face of possibility.

One can see then how and why Heidegger can speak of the "existential project of death." Any project that Dasein could undertake rests upon a prior understanding of it as possible, which in turn rests upon a prior relation toward possibility as such. The ultimate, prior relation to possibility as such is nothing else but Dasein's relation to its own death: "death is the horizon of projection within which all projects are made possible."[24] In addition, in its most intensified form, death not only grounds projects, but can itself become a project: the essential project of Dasein. Heidegger works out various modalities internal to this project—most importantly, "resolutenesss"—but its actual course involves Dasein's holding itself open to the decisive affective dimension in relation to death: *anxiety*. "In anxiety, Dasein finds itself faced with the nothingnesss of the possible impossibility of its existence."[25] To exist authentically in care, to take up death as a project, is thus to fully inhabit the anxiety in terms of which one is brought before oneself as much as brought before one's own death.

Being-together-with-death *contra* being-toward-death

To return to Kierkegaard: does Kierkegaard's discourse on death present the listener with a *project* of death, or present death as a project? Does death accomplish a similar function as in Heidegger's analysis: namely, putting the self in touch with possibility as such and thus ecstatically opening the self to the world in which it can seize possibilities—up to and including the possibility of seizing itself in its possible being? *Is death the foundation of meaning*?

As I will argue, Heidegger's systematic reinscription of death through the structure of care—and thus, finally, in its relation to the irruption of the horizon of temporality—in fact displaces the central problematic of death in Kierkegaard's discourse. Heidegger treats death in two fundamentally different registers: as the total negation of Dasein, an interruption of its being that is absolute; *and* as Dasein's eminent possibility, something taken up as the foundation of all its projects. In the end, though, it is the latter understanding of death that Heidegger makes foundational—which is to say, he makes care and consequently the project the foundational structure of Dasein. Death is ceded productive power and its absolutely interruptive character—by which, according to Kierkegaard, "meaning is banished"—is occluded. The lynchpin in Heidegger's argument is in placing the mood of anxiety as what supposedly brings one before death in an original, authentic way. In anxiety an absolute interruption—the breaking off of all project structures—is replaced by the "possibility of possibility"—which is to say, the *ground* of all projects. The logic here is familiar: in place of a rupture, a ground. Heidegger thinks death metaphysically. The fundamental falsification in his account is to substitute or the negation of possibility as such for my "ownmost possibility not-to-be-bypassed."

And, in fact, anxiety before death is characteristic only of those who are not actually facing death; it is the healthy who are anxious before death and who have the luxury of thinking of death as their ownmost eminent possibility. Death-as-possibility, as the horizon of the possible, is but life's self-projection as infinite. Life before "death's decision" faces an absolute interruption, a possibility that *cannot* be taken up in care—not even a possibility, not even the impossibility of possibility, but the pure annihilation of possibility. Life before death's decision is thrust outside the horizon of care.

In being-toward-death, temporality signifies the way Dasein is always *on its way* toward achieving its wholeness. Time temporalizes out of the future and Dasein is essentially project. In the relation being "*together* with death," by contrast, time is endowed with a wholly different sense. The originary relation with death is not temporal but spatial: death is proximate, close by—not impending but impinging. Death does not approach via the distance of the future and therefore is not mediated by the mood of anxiety. When death is made proximate time appears, for the first time, as a precious resource not to be wasted. Death's proximity does not make one anxious, but makes one "wide awake" (*aarvaagen*): "for death in seriousness gives life force as nothing else; it makes one wakeful as nothing else does."[26] Time is not the horizon within which the self understands itself as always ahead of itself, but appears rather as, so to speak, a *commodity* susceptible to scarcity: "Time is also a good (*et Gode*);"[27] and "death itself produces a scarcity of time (*Dyrtid paa Tid*)."[28]

That is the fundamental function of death in relation to time: to make time appear as what it is—namely, as finite—a circumstance, however, that endows time with "infinite worth." Time is worth something only as finite, as absolutely revocable. In the thought of death time appears as what will always be cut off *in midstream*. Rather than negate the meaning or worth of time, however, this fosters a sense of time—of each moment—as of infinite worth. In proximity to the interruption of death, each moment is endowed with the remarkable character of being at once essentially complete and essentially incomplete. The moment does not gain its worth and reality, in other words, as part of a larger whole: to the contrary, the moment is fully real *as* incomplete. *Only as incomplete*. Thus the project structure is banished. In place of the "existential project of death" Kierkegaard enunciates the "essential work" of life. The latter is not defined by its end-goal or completion, but receives its meaning solely through its beginning. The sole goal of the essential work is to strike upon the beginning in the right way—which means, to undertake those things that can be complete in their very incompletion. Whatever such things may be, they are definitely not projects. Such things retain their entire worth in their incipience. Kierkegaard writes: "but the essential work is not defined essentially by time and the external, insofar as death is the interruption. Seriousness, therefore, becomes the living of each day as if it were the last and also the first in a long life and the choosing of work that depend on whether one is granted a lifetime to complete it well or only a brief time to have begun it well."[29]

In this way death, precisely as interruption, exercises a "retroactive force" upon life. This force propels the person, not ecstatically toward the future in project, but toward the present itself, toward the task of taking one's measure from the present. Kierkegaard writes: "But the thought of death gives the serious person the right speed in life and the right measure (*det rette Maal*) by which to direct it."[30] Death insists: the proper measure of human existence is to be found in the present moment itself, nowhere else. The thought of death allows one to measure the quality of effort, how one is using time.

Conclusion: even so, today

Between death and the serious thought of death there takes place a small dialogue: "When death comes, the word is: up to here, not one step further ... all is over."[31] In response life utters its own logos: "Even so, today'" (*Endu i Dag*). The Danish expression *Endu i Dag* is complex and resists translation.[32] Its basic sense is to indicate that the day is nevertheless *still* there—even after, and despite, its end. In other words, the present itself appears a surprise, a superfluity, which *therefore* can be put to gratuitous use. Seriousness, facing up to pure annihilation, grasps the present in its precise quality as remainder, as what still persists and can be used, even if, and after, "all is over."

PART THREE

BLOOMINGS: DISCOURSES ON "THE LILY OF THE FIELD AND THE BIRD OF THE AIR" (1847, 1849)

7

Against care: discourses on the lilies of the field and the birds of the air (1847)[1]

There are several New Testament texts that Kierkegaard showed a particular attraction to, texts he returned to on multiple occasions. One of those texts is from *The Gospel of Matthew*: "Consider the lilies of the field and the birds of the air." Indeed Kierkegaard wrote two small books on this one passage, in 1847 and 1849. I will focus on the 1847 discourses and argue that in these discourses Kierkegaard is centrally concerned with the problem of "being human." We are encouraged "to be content with being human" (first discourse) to reflect upon "the glory of being human" (second discourse) and to consider the happiness that is promised to us in being human (third discourse). What it is to be human is at stake here.

Indeed, what I would like to suggest is that across these discourses Kierkegaard succeeds in interrogating the being of the human being, that is, in raising an ontological problematic. Drawing upon a long tradition that originates in Paul (and that includes also Hegel) Kierkegaard names the being of the human being by the term "spirit" (*Aand*). What is interesting, however, is that Kierkegaard clarifies the meaning of spirit by reference to that which is, apparently, not at all spirit: the lily of the field and the bird of the air. They are to instruct us in what it is to be human. There is a paradox here: the lily of the field and the bird of the air lack what might seem, from the standpoint of the idealist metaphysics of modernity, at least, to constitute the unique ontological structure of the human: consciousness or, more precisely, *self-consciousness*. From Descartes through the various permutations of idealism—from Kant through Fichte and Hegel—the ontological specificity of the human being was understood in terms of the power to achieve and remain present to oneself, to present oneself before oneself, to *represent* oneself. This milieu of representation was considered a privileged domain of the real. Indeed, the milieu of representation was understood as that within which and upon the basis of which anything could become present at all. The gambit of idealist metaphysics was to justify self-consciousness as the *ground* of the real.

In these discourses on the lily of the field and the bird of the air Kierkegaard abruptly displaces this idealist problematic in order, as it were, to begin all over again. To grasp who we are, to come to terms with the being of our being, it is not adequate to retrace the ways and powers of consciousness, of representation, to render the real present. We must consider the lily of the field and the bird of the air; we must look to *that which has no interiority at all*. The blooming lily, the bird in flight, show forth an ontological dimension of the human being that is not, and cannot be, grasped in the terms of an idealist metaphysics.

What they show to us according to Kierkegaard, I will suggest, is a dimension of "whylessness" or, if one likes, "anarchy"—namely a dimension refractory to projects, reasons, principles, goals. The lily blooms because it blooms, without its blooming becoming a project; and the bird of the air "neither sows nor reaps nor gathers into barns," it does not establish itself economically. According to these discourses the human being exists according to its deepest possibility, as spirit, only when it achieves a comportment in its existence isomorphic to the lily and the bird. Kierkegaard summarizes the whole trajectory of these discourses as follows: "only when the human being, though he works and spins, is just like the lily, which does not work or spin, only when the human being, although he sows and reaps and gathers into barns, is just like the bird, which does not sow and reap and gather into barns, only then does he [exist according to his possibility as spirit]."[2]

I will proceed by considering each discourse in turn. All together, the three discourses constitute the progressive deepening of a problematic.

First discourse: the initial critique of care as an ultimate ontological structure

If these discourses involve a critical problematic directed against the metaphysics of representation, it is important to note that they engage this problematic in a concrete mode: namely, as a critique of concern or care (*Sorg*). The human being is, concretely, the being who is always already wrapped up in concerns—first and foremost in the concern to procure the material conditions of existence, what in Danish is called *Næringsorg* (literally, the concern for nutriments and alimentation). *Næringsorg* is the most basic modality of *Sorg*. The lily of the field and the bird, however, exist without concern: and not just as a matter of fact, but for essential reasons. In terms of the being of the lily and the bird there is no possibility of forming concern. And why not? Because the lily and the bird belong wholly to the moment, to the Now, in such a total way that it cannot even be called a "Now." They exist "without temporality's foresight, unaware of time, in the moment."[3] The birth of concern in the human being, therefore, is linked to the upsurge of a temporal consciousness. Only a being whose existence is constituted on the horizon of temporality can, in general, become concerned. Time consciousness constitutes the general conditions for the possibility of concern.

The human being, unlike the lily and the bird, exists on the basis of a power of temporal projection, what Kierkegaard calls *Forsynlighedens Arbeiden*—that is, to translate it literally, the work of anticipative foresight. This work, the primordial labor of the human being, involves the synthesis of three modalities of time: past, present and future. Speaking of the man of concern Kierkegaard writes:

> When on the basis of a *past time* he has filled his hoppers, and is therefore provisioned for the *present time*, then he takes care to sow again for the future harvest, so that he can again fill his hoppers for the *future time*. For this reason three words are used to indicate the labor of anticipative foresight ... and the three words indicate the determination of time, which constitues the ground of anticipation (*Forsynligheden*).[4]

Forsynligheden, the power of consciousness to project a temporal horizon, the gathering together of past, present and future in a dilated present, constitutes the explicitly articulated foundation of concern.

As an abrupt contrast to what appears fundamental to human reality, however, Kierkegaard says of the lily and the bird: they "do not labor"—*de arbeider ikke*. In context this means precisely that they do not engage in the labor of projecting time. They belong to the moment but do not constitute the moment. They exist purely in the moment without any temporal ecstasy and, for this exact reason, they exist outside of the structure of concern—not merely contingently, but essentially, that is, outside the very *possibility* of forming concerns. Only on the basis of a consciousness of time and therefore on the basis of the labor of consciousness involved in the formation of temporal ecstases *can* one have a concern. Concern is conditioned, in terms of its possibility, by the constitution of a temporal consciousness and the lily and the bird do not labor.

Moreover, according to Kierkegaard the projection of time is in fact but one of the modalities of a more basic power: the power of representation. Time consciousness arises only in and through the more general power of representation, something that belongs to and makes up the reality of consciousness. Human reality plays out, in fundamental and ineluctable ways, on the plane of representation. If the lily and the bird have no concern, this is because they do not exist within a horizon of temporality; and if they do not exist within a horizon of temporality, this is because they belong to the moment without having constituted the moment through their own labor, that is, through the spontaneity of their own consciousness. The human being, however, exists on the basis of a strange aporia: the present moment, what seems always original, is in fact the *outcome* of a previous work: the present is in fact a recapturing of presence, thus a re-presenting. Thus the present has the quality of being, in some way, secondary or delayed. Without this gap or delay there could be no distance from the present and, thus, no possibility of constituting a dilated present that includes the past and the future. The whole plane of representation, the human plane, thus plays out at a certain essential remove from the real. The lily and the bird belong to the real without distance; not so the human being.

Insofar as the human being exists on the basis of a power of representation and thus does not immediately belong to the real, another modality of its life—one that relates intimately to concern—becomes possible: what Kierkegaard calls "comparison" (*Sammenligningen*). Comparison, a power founded in representation, is a fecund source of concern. Kierkegaard says "*Næringsorg* comes into being by means of comparsion."[5] And it does so in a double way: first, existing with one another, speaking and taking notice of each other, human beings fashion comparative terms within which to understand themselves. An essential possibility for human beings, one that does not pertain to the lily and the bird, is to "not be contented with being human," that is, to exist on the basis of a represented lack. Kierkegaard explores the folly of a human life consumed by the sense of lack, in a humorous vein, by imagining a lily comparing itself (negatively) to a Crown Imperial flower and a wild wood dove comparing itself to a well-fed domesticated dove. In each case they are completely consumed by the sense of lack and, aiming to overcome lack, they perish: the lily becomes uprooted and the wood dove becomes the farmer's dinner. If we smile at the lily and the bird in this case, Kierkegaard suggests, we are only smiling at our own folly; we are acknowledging our own entanglement in representations.

In a deeper and more intimate way, however, comparison transpires in and through the consciousness of time: where the present acquires its meaning (or has its meaning evacuated) through a comparison with the future. In these terms, concern arises as founded upon the "*representation* of need in the future." Kierkegaard writes: "comparison constitutes the ground of *Næringsorg* insofar as this latter does not express an actual, but a represented need."[6] The future arises through the projective power of consciousness and thus has the ontological status of a representation; the future has no actuality. And yet, through comparison, this represented reality is allowed to determine the reality of the present. It is there one finds the upsurge of concern and, in concern, the peeling apart of the human being from its own moment, its own reality, and thus its subjection to the vast world of lack. Again, the lily and the bird form the abrupt contrast: "How is it that the bird has no *Næringsorg*? For this reason: that it does not compare one day with another."[7]

Against the representation of future lack, along with the concern it generates, human labor must dedicate itself to "storing up in barns," that is, to stockpiling capital as a hedge against the future. Thus, the primary laboring of fashioning a consciousness of time constitutes the condition for what in the broader sense is called economic life. Human labor always already transpires in a domain of political economy where the value of labor and the value of commodities produced have the status of representations. Human life itself becomes predicated upon relations of comparison: comparing one day to the next, one person to another, one thing with another thing. None of the comparisons is ontologically founded, and yet—in terms of political economy—they do constitute the very reality of human life. There is the rub, there is the bottomless source of concern. For Marx, there is the bottomless possibility of a disfigured social and human existence.

The realm of concern, then, coincides in an interesting way with the realm of what Marx called "ideology:" that which is in essence representational comes to determine actuality. As Kierkegaard puts it, the central problem is the possibility of becoming *self-ensnared* in our own representations. Only the human being, who exists precisely on the plane of representation, can entrap *itself*. Thus Kierkegaard says that the concerned one has "entrapped himself in the snare ... in which only the free [human being] can ensnare himself: in representation."[8] It is something remarkable: we are able to ensnare ourselves in comparative categories and in temporal projections. All of the concerns of human beings have their origin in this possibility of self-ensnarement. Things that are not real, things we present to ourselves as real—abstract notions like "tomorrow" or "wages"—for human beings constitute the very domain of the real. Existing with one another, we speak, and in speaking we fashion comparative terms—abstract categories—within which we then understand ourselves. This world of concern is an inverted world: the represented becomes the most real and the most real can appear to us only in a figure—namely, in terms of the being of the lily and the bird. The passage back to reality for the human being, then, involves a movement beyond representation, a comportment in existence that does not rely upon projections that have their origin in our free spontaneity. In this, the lily of the field and the bird of the air can be our teachers.

And yet, is there not a problem here? Is there not an ontological chasm between human reality, which exists always upon the basis of representation, and the lily and the bird, who do not? Does not this divide preclude any essential instruction? Are we lilies? Are we birds?

Now, the first discourse, which we must remember is written in a comic mode, sends us out into the fields to look at the lily and the bird. Why out into the fields? Precisely because "out there" human life is not organized by an economy founded in representation. "Out there" the lily blooms and the bird takes wing wholly in the instant itself, in the joyous upsurge of being, without fashioning any abstract, comparative terms within which to live. If we imagine the lily and the bird living in terms of comparative terms, living through representations of future lack, we smile. But if we smile, Kierkegaard suggests, we are only smiling at ourselves—smiling at our own comical conflation of the real and the representation of the real. The point of the first discourse, however, is only initially to open up the distinction between something like the real and the representational order. To pay attention to the lily and the bird allows, for the person suffering concern, a momentary lifting of the reign of comparative terms and the burdens of temporality. Seeing the representational status of the terms in which we live, we are free of their tyranny. "Out there" we get what is called "perspective." Yet this is only momentary. The human problem goes deeper and requires a deeper reflection.

Discourse 2: spirit as capability

The second discourse comes to grip with the fact that temporality, labor and comparison—in general, the whole order of representation—belongs essentially to the human condition. It seeks to clarify the ontological chasm that separates human reality from the joyous kingdom of being of the lily and the bird. Human reality is characterized by an essential ambiguity: to be *capable* of labor, *capable* of constituting a time consciousness, *capable* of representation, these constitute the "glory" of the human; nevertheless, such capability constitutes also the conditions for the possibility of a destitution, misery and illusion that are never found in the joyous kingdom of nature. The second discourse is dedicated to the clarification of this ambiguity. And here it becomes clear that the lily and the bird cannot, in the strictest sense, be our teachers. Nevertheless, we can still learn from the lily and the bird.

What is important about the lily and the bird in the second discourse is that, in spite of their difference from the human, they are nevertheless, through a contrast, able to bring human beings to the contemplation of their own "glory." Concretely, to be human is to be mired in the concerns and comparative categories that belong to temporal existence. In the concrete sense, the terms by which human beings affirm themselves are comparative and relative. And yet, according to Kierkegaard, this is where the lily and the bird can intervene in order to reorganize the human gaze upon itself. The second discourse begins by comparing concern to a fixed stare: "How could one better indicate how concern takes root in the soul than by saying that it is like the eye which *stares*. When the eye stares it gazes fixedly ahead of itself, seeing only one thing, though in fact not seeing anything, since as the scientist explains it sees its own seeing. But then the physician says: move the eye."[9] In concern the gaze fixates upon the blank nothing of the future. Though it appears to be seeing something, in fact it is seeing only its own seeing. Concern, in other words, is a modality of self-consciousness. In concern the human being rotates upon himself, immersing himself in his own projections, even while seeming to look outward. The "cure" for this is to move the eye—that is, to reorient the quality of attention, to reorganize the gaze, and in such a way that there is an exit from self-consciousness. The lily and the bird, in their manifestness, serve as a catalyst for this movement.

What the lily and the bird can do, in particular, is to bring the human being to what Kierkegaard calls that "first thought" (*Første Tanken*), that is, to an affirmation of itself that is naïve, or non-comparative. The lily and the bird can provoke the human to see itself through itself, as a genuine phenomenon, in the original naïveté of its reality, liberated from the accumulated ideas of what it is to be human. The lily and the bird can provoke what Husserl later called an "epoché of the natural attitude."

Take the lily, which is arrayed in a glorious raiment. Kierkegaard says of the lily: "it is said that the lily is arrayed, but this is not to be understood in such a way that the lily's existence is one thing and the fact of having raiment is something different; no, its raiment is the being lily itself."[10] The lily exhausts the whole plenitude of its being in manifesting itself; it is nothing other than its self-manifesting. Or, to put it differently, the lily *is* the blooming of the lily, something like a pure surface, an outside with no inside. The lily, to put it in the terms Kierkegaard uses, belongs entirely to the order of *the visible*. Its glory is a visible glory.

Now, here is why we can learn from the lily: the lily can teach us what it means to look at a phenomenon. Having learned what it means to see from the show of the lily the human being can bring this same gaze upon himself—namely, to regard his own being as clothing, as glorious raiment, as a phenomenon. Kierkegaard writes: "Being clothed means then being human—and so to be well-clothed."[11] The lily can awaken us again, we who are burdened by concern and enmeshed in comparative categories, to that basic posture of *wonder* in which we pay attention only, as it were, to the outward show of the thing, to the immediate blazing forth of the thing as the thing it is. The profoundest gaze upon the lily is not the gaze of the scientist, interested for example in a comparative taxonomy of lilies. No, the profoundest gaze is one which sees in the lily nothing more than its raiment, nothing more than a surface to take delight in. The lily becomes an object of wonder, and wonder is the form of attention which lets a thing show itself as the thing it is.

As we look at the lily, we might look at ourselves. For the human being too, our "raiment," in other words the being of our being, is something that can manifest itself to our naïve gaze. In the biblical language Kierkegaard draws upon, this will say that the being of our being has the ontological status of an *image*—we are, namely, made in "the image of God." If our being has the ontological status of an image, that means it belongs, like the being of the lily, to the order of the visible. Indeed, to speak of the glory of the human being is already to situate human beings with respect to the visible, since glory is a category of the visible, of the manifest. And yet, here is where Kierkegaard's discourse takes a turn, where the phenomenology becomes radicalized. For the human being Kierkegaard finds its necessary to speak, paradoxically, of an "invisible glory." He says: "To be spirit, that is the human being's invisible glory."[12] The glory of the lily is a purely visible glory; the glory of the human an invisible one. Therefore, to affirm the human being in a naïve way, to remain in that "first thought" about the human, will be to affirm a dimension of invisibility as what essentially belongs to the human. And yet, paradoxically, this invisibility can itself become a phenomenon to the extent that the being of the human is an "image."

It is, on the one hand, the insignia of the human being's ontological specificity as spirit that, in some way, the human being resembles God; a lily, by contrast, does not. And yet, on the other hand, Kierkegaard does something quite interesting with this traditional motif: if one is to speak of the human being as an image of God, it is necessary to think about an image in a way entirely different than a representation. Generally an image, thought as a representation, is poor in being, a copy, a reflection, a lack; it acquires its reality from something external to it. Kierkegaard writes: "When a person sees his image in the mirror of the ocean, he sees his own image, but the ocean is not his image, and when he departs the image disappears. The ocean is not the image and cannot keep the image. Why is this, except for the reason that the visible form by its very visibility is powerless."[13] That which is visible can manifest itself only in a medium other than itself. The visible image is for this reason emptied out of its own reality, characterized by essential lack. Human reality, however, does not belong to the plane of the visible, but rather the invisible. In other words, if we resemble God, it cannot be through any property of ourselves that belongs to the order of the visible.

What Kierkegaard's discourse invites us to do is to look at the entire dimension of human lack, the whole realm of human errancy, of concern, as expressive of the glory of the human being. For underneath the human being's exposure to itself, underneath its forming of concern, underneath its establishment of representation as the domain of the real, there is the fundamental ontological power of the human being: being able (*at kunne*).

Only the human being is capable of erring, capable of concern, capable of representation. This, its capability, is its glory. Capability, being able as such, is our raiment, our invisible glory. So, for example: to live a life burdened by the concern over procuring the conditions of existence, a life consumed by labor aimed at protecting oneself against some represented future need, such a life is not a perfection. The lily and the bird are perfect in being free of concern and labor. Nevertheless, Kierkegaard says, the *capability* of having concern, the *capability* of labor, these are, *thought purely as capabilities*, perfections.

But the dimension of capability, the dimension of spirit, is fundamentally invisible. How so? Kierkegaard asks: "How is it that concern is possible?" In other words, how are we capable of concern? He answers: "Only by the fact that the eternal and the temporal touch each other in a consciousness; or, more correctly, that the human being has consciousness. In consciousness he is far, far above the instant, no bird flew so high up."[14] The lily and the bird belong so wholly to the instant, to the Now, that it cannot even be called a Now. They belong to a plane of pure presence. It is precisely because they inhabit this plane of presence that they have no capability and, to be precise, that they are unable to form any concern. The human being, the being who is capable, on the other hand, both inhabits the instant and also stands far, far above it. In other words, the human being is the being that is always already divided from itself, incapable of being at one with itself. Thus, human capability originates in this radical incapability, in this rift or fracture, this rupture from immediacy. The dimension of invisibility that constitutes the very glory of the human being, then, is its reference to this gap in presence. Not belonging to the plane of presence constitutes the conditioning possibility of the human being.

Thus the glory of the human is caught sight of inversely through the possibility of suffering all the excesses of consciousness: for example, boredom and concern over the future. Even more deeply, human glory shines inversely in the possibility of extreme destitution and misery, as in the New Testament saying that the "son of man has no place to lay his head"—something that can never be said of the bird or the lily. Only the human being can really suffer this essential placelessness. Placelessness is not itself a perfection, of course, but the possibility of not belonging to place is a perfection, the very perfection of spirit. Only the human is *able* to lack place. The divine image constitutive of human reality is, again, essentially invisible.

It is only through this originary rupture from the plane of presence, then, that the human being has capability at all. The divine image is invisible. Only through its not being at one with itself can the human being, in the strictest sense, become something. The human being, to put it precisely, is the *being who is capable of becoming*. However, the way Kierkegaard develops this problematic in this discourse is to say that the human being is the only being who is capable of worship: "in truth to be able to worship is the invisible glory of the human above all other creatures."[15]

The capability to "worship," then, summarizes the very meaning of human capability and thus marks the distinction between the human and the lily and the bird. In the naïveté of their being the lily and the bird are "atheist." So what, then, is worship *thought as a pure capability*? Kierkegaard contrasts the Christian point of view to that of the Greeks. The Greeks, he says, saw the glory of the human being in the erect posture and in the gaze of the eye. In other words, the Greeks understood the being of the human being in the power of *theoria*, intellectual vision, and in the exercise of sovereignty. Standing above the elements, commanding them, ruling, constitutes Greek glory. For Kierkegaard, this was still to think of the human in terms of a visible glory—that is, in terms of a capability exercised wholly upon the plane of the visible. It does not come to terms, in other words, with the decisive, ontological dimension of the human being.

To be exact, it does not grasp the nature of the becoming that is proper to the human being. Worship grasps this capability, this becoming. But the crux of worship is the following: "It is glorious to be arrayed like the lily; even more glorious to be the ruler who stands erect; but it is most glorious to be nothing through the act of worship."[16] Only the human being is the being who is capable of grasping his own nothingness, of entering into and assuming that nothingness. Becoming nothing is the way of human becoming. Only the human being can see and experience and consent to its own non-sovereignty, its inability to posit being or to posit itself in being. To worship, thought as a capability, thus turns around to become the capability of not being able. Worship signifies the human capacity to see its capability as something for which it is not capable. Thus, returning to the lily and to the reorganization of the gaze, Kierkegaard writes: "if a human being is going to compare himself to the lily, he has to say: All that I am by being a human being—that is my clothing; none of it is owing to myself, and yet it is glorious."[17] Capability is indeed the human being's *own* capability; and yet the human does not, as Fichte would have it, posit itself as capable.

Discourse three: decision as radical capability

According to the second discourse the glory of the human being lies in its capabilities. In the third discourse Kierkegaard tries to clarify a further element of capability, that of choice or decision. Being able to choose constitutes the glory of the human and separates the human from the lily and the bird, whose existence plays out on a plane of necessity. And as Kierkegaard will say, the only real choice is the choice between "God" and "mammon." We shall have to see what this choice means.

In the third discourse there is a definite shift of focus. Kierkegaard considers the being of the lily and the being of the bird with respect to what might be called the general economy of nature. In the order of nature, life and death are tragically conjoined, to the point of identity. The death of one thing is already the beginning of something else, the making room for, enabling, fertilizing some other thing. Life and death are so inseparably joined in nature that it becomes impossible to say what power is actually manifest in nature. Of the blooming lily, Kierkegaard asks, with the full pathos of a lacuna: "*is it life or is it death?*" When a lily blooms in all its splendor, he continues, is this "the life which, eternally young, renews itself, or is it the corruption which treacherously conceals itself?"[18] What power is it, exactly, that manifests itself in the blooming of the lily? Is it life or death? Is it natality or mortality? Can one even answer this question? Is it even intelligible to speak of a difference?

The impossibility of any resolution to this question, of any disjoining of life and death, is what Kierkegaard calls the "corruptibility" of nature. All things, human and inhuman, are subject to corruption. However, there is already something different happening in the human: it is the human being who is capable of asking "is it life or is it death?" At the site of the human, the site of spirit, things do not merely expend themselves, they are "recollected" in the fragility of a trace. The general economy of nature is, as it were, upset or suspended in recollection: things do not just pass, they linger. Last summer's lilies, once in bloom but now no more (never more, as Poe would say), yet bloom still in recollection. This lingering of things prior to their annihilation is what Kierkegaard calls *Veemod*, melancholy. Melancholy to this extent constitutes the very structure of consciousness; and it is as though melancholy were already the beginnings of something different, a different kind of blooming altogether. And indeed for Kierkegaard it is.

Melancholy is the intensification of concern. Or rather, it is already a rupture of all the structures of concern inasmuch as it is the gripping of the human being by an essential indetermination. Melancholy constitutes the very resonance of the question: is it life or is it death? In melancholy the meaning of being becomes questionable and so calls forth, according to Kierkegaard, a fundamental decision, a choice. And here we gain a sense of the specific meaning of the capability of the human, that which constitutes its invisible glory: the capability for a radical decision. The lily of the field and the bird of the air play out their whole being, Kierkegaard says, on a plane of necessity, without choice. The human being is the being who must decide concerning the meaning of its being. Melancholy is the crisis which calls forth a decision.

So what sort of decision is at issue here? Kierkegaard formulates the terms of this choice by drawing upon the language of the New Testament: it is a choice between "God" and "mammon." He writes: "The human being must choose between God and mammon. This is the eternal, unalterable condition of choice."[19] The lily and the bird do not possess this capability of choice; it is the glory of the human. However, it is necessary to ask, what is this choice between God and mammon? Why is it that Kierkegaard formulates the question of the meaning of being as a choice between God and mammon? Is this not arbitrary? And, just to make explicit an issue that might arise, does not this appeal to God involve precisely an abandonment of the question of being? Does Kierkegaard not explicitly adopt a mode of thinking that must be called ontotheological, namely, a thinking that tries to secure the meaning of being by representing the highest instance of being (namely, God) as the ground of being and reason for being? Aren't we dealing with the terrain of representations on literally the highest level? Though Kierkegaard without a doubt inherits a certain discourse on God, what is necessary is to examine the text itself.

First of all, the choice between God and mammon is not a choice between one thing and another thing. God is not present to the choice simply as an object of choice, but rather as the very condition of choosing. Kierkegaard says: "God's presence in the choice [is what] posits the choice—between God and mammon."[20] One could say that, more basically than some thing chosen, God constitutes for Kierkegaard this persistent structural possibility of choosing. God is the name for the rift which involves the human being in a choice concerning the meaning of its being. In addition, to choose God is not to choose some ultimate object, but rather to choose a certain way of being. This is why one is dealing here with what might be called a fundamental choice, a choice that bears upon *how* I will be in each moment. By the very nature of such a choice it is something that is chosen "first." Or, in the biblical language

Kierkegaard appeals to, it is necessary to "seek *first* the kingdom of God." Kierkegaard underscores the originary nature of the choice.

So, God/mammon, the choice of the world, or of the kingdom of God, these are the terms of a radical choice, where the being of the human being is at stake, which is to say its most basic comportment. To choose *first* the kingdom of God is the New Testament name for this comportment. So again, what is it to choose God?

Over several pages Kierkegaard works out a series of substitutions on the name "God," which I summarize as follows: to choose God, he says, means to choose "the kingdom of God;" and to choose the kingdom of God means to choose the justice that belongs to this kingdom, God's "righteousness;" and to chose the justice that belongs to this kingdom is to choose, Kierkegaard says, to "remain in one's place" (*bliver paa Stedet*). Kierkegaard writes: "while then the visible world is destroyed and sinks in corruption, *then you still remain in your place*, and the beginning is first to seek the kingdom of God." He continues: "but if it is true that the whole visible world is to sink in corruption, then the human being has no other point to which he can flee, and precisely for that reason he remains at that place."[21] At what place? At the place where the human belongs in the totality of its being to the corruptibility of all things.

Consequently, to choose God, to seek God's kingdom first, signifies for the human being *to consent to its place*, that is, to its belonging to the order of total corruptibility, to consent with absolutely no reservations. The lily of the field and the bird of the air remain ever "in place." Even the bird, though in constant movement, never really moves since it never moves outside its own "Now." Only the human being can move, can become, and to become means precisely here to *become finite*, to *assume* or take on corruptibility as a condition. Only the human being can actually enter into its own finitude. To assume the condition of finitude, to remain in place, is simultaneously to open oneself to the gratuity of life. It is to learn to see life itself as what has the structure of a "remainder"—Kierkegaard uses the Danish word "*det Øvrige*"—namely as excess, as what overflows beyond any necessity. The being of the human being, then, is that site in being where the gratuity of being can be marked. This is the meaning of spirit.

Concluding preface: becoming a lily

In conclusion I want to return to the question of how the human being can, in its own way, become lily-like and bird-like. As Kierkegaard said: "only when the human being, though he toils and spins, is absolutely like the lily, which does not toil and spin; only when the human being, although he sows and reaps and gathers into barns, is absolutely like the bird, which does not sow and reap and gather into barns, only then does he not serve mammon." To serve mammon is to organize one's existence around the project, which is to say in terms of final ends and on the basis of future possibilities which originate in the representational power of consciousness. Serving mammon only has a sense within a horizon constituted by concern.

The movement of Kierkegaard's discourses, however, have disclosed a dimension of capability that is prior to that of concern. And then again, going even further, have disclosed a dimension of radical incapability underneath capability as its conditioning possibility (no one gives capability to themselves). Finally, they have pointed to an expression of this capability—decision—which no longer has anything like the project about it. To choose the justice that belongs to the kingdom of God is to remain at, or enter into, one's place. This is justice as adjustment, as a being situated. It is entering into one's own site, one's own givenness. Nothing is produced in this labor; it is labor as expenditure, without finality—and to this extent, it passes over from labor, organized around ends, into something like growth (lily) or flight (bird).

In conclusion, let us ask: what kind of existence is this? How is it that a human being can achieve a comportment that is lily-like and bird-like? What would it mean to exist no longer on the basis of concern, without project? What would a relation to the real be that is unmediated by representation? Actually, these have been persistent questions in the Western tradition, or at least within a certain stratum of that tradition. To be specific, Kierkegaard's discourses must finally be understood in terms of a problematic inaugurated by Marguerite Porete and Meister Eckhart, according to which only that which lives "without a why" truly lives.[22] This tradition reemerges with great force, even if in a transformed way, in the later thought of Heidegger.[23]

In order to sketch the direction of such a thought, and without being able to address Kierkegaard's relations to these thinkers here, it would be most appropriate to turn to the preface to *What We Learn from the Lilies of the Field and the Birds of the Air*. The preface opens a path, not only of reading, but also already of existence. Kierkegaard writes:

> Although this little book is without the *authority* of the teacher, [is] a *superfluity, insignificant,* like the lily and the bird—Oh, if only it were so!—it nevertheless hopes that by finding the only thing it seeks, a good place, it finds the *significance of appropriation* for that singular one whom I, with gladness and gratitude, call *my* reader.[24]

Already contained in this preface is a certain circularity that relates to the reading of the text: the book is to guide human beings into a comportment that is lily-like and bird-like, and yet it can only be read appropriately—that is, in such a way as to allow it to find *its* place—on condition that one is already able to grasp lily-being and bird-being. But this means already having become lily-like and bird-like. The book presupposes in the reader, in other words, the very comportment to which it wants to lead the reader. It presupposes that the reader is already capable of grasping the significance of that which has no significance, of that which in its very being is superfluous. The book itself, ontologically, is a bird, a lily; and it arises out of a posture that is lily-like and bird-like. Therefore it can only be read appropriately—which means here *appropriatively*—out of a prior sensitivity to the superfluous and insignificant. In other words, the very structure of the book presupposes that there is something already within the existence of the reader that is receptive to that which overflows economies of meaning and acting-for-ends. So it is not really a question of "how to become a lily or a bird;" rather, it is about allowing this dimension of anarchy, what *already* structures life prior to and after the mediations of self-consciousness, greater place.

8

Lily-bird-being/joy without condition: *The lily of the field and the bird of the air* (1849)

Three times Kierkegaard wrote a series of discourses using Matthew 6:24–34 as the locus of his reflection: as part two of *Upbuilding Discourses in Various Spirits* (1847), as the central text in "The Cares of the Pagans" in *Christian Discourses* (1848), and finally as its own small book, titled *The Lily of the Field and the Bird of the Air: Three Divine Discourses* (1849). At stake in these discourses is a steadily deepening critique of care (*Sorg*) or concern (*Bekymring*).

As already indicated, Kierkegaard's situates his critique of care at the ontological level—that is to say, with respect to a consideration of the being of the human being. The structure of care is ultimately identical to the structure of the project, which in turn receives its foundation in the generalized power of "representation" (*Forestillingen*), that is, the power of the self to maintain its presence to itself across a temporal duration and to understand itself in terms of ends held anticipatively in view. More deeply, its project character means, to borrow a suitable phrase from Heidegger, the self's being is "always at issue for it," that it exists as "being-ahead-of-itself," pressing into its possibilities. The radical basis in terms of which care appears as ultimate—in Heidegger as well as in Kierkegaard's discourses—is the conception of the self (Heidegger's Dasein) in terms of a fundamental "I Can."[1] Kierkegaard's critique of care, therefore, centers on identifying that ontological power in terms of which the being of the human being is adequately conceived: it consists in showing the derivative nature of the "I Can." It consists in showing how human capability (*Formaaen*) can in no wise be conceived through or out of itself; that instead it refers to an *incapability* that is absolute. The self finds itself always already involved in self, possessed of self, riveted to itself. This deeper structure of incapability vis-à-vis itself points to a dimension of its being—its "inner" being—that is in principle refractory to the project. No project can un-rivet the self from itself, even if it be the "existential project of death;" there is no project of self-overcoming. And yet there is self-overcoming through the overcoming of the structures of the self: namely, representation, care and project. It goes without saying that the self itself cannot constitute the origin of these destructions.

The three "divine discourses" in the *Lily of the Field and the Bird of the Air* take up this exceptionally difficult problem: what are the inner determinations of the way of being, of the basic attunement, in which the self exists without care? What are the conditions for the possibility of an existence that has altogether found its *time* and its *place* and consequently exists "without tomorrow," in a condition of being-present-to-itself? It is a matter of existing in terms of a joy (*Glæde*) that is altogether without conditions, a joy over nothing. More fundamentally than care, the relation that transpires between the human being and being, and consequently the event that defines the being of the human being, is joy. Joy is thus not an isolated emotion, but the very relation to being, a name for the inception of being itself. The lily of the field and the bird of the air, Kierkegaard says, are our "master teachers" in this regard: being "joy itself," they teach joy. They become the very emblems through which the human being is able to move, in an extraordinary movement, "backwards to the beginning," toward the affirmation "there is a today" (*det er et i Dag*). "Today" would be the time-place at once closest and the most distant.

Discourse I: the living being with language

Silence as the condition of speech: poetic attunement

Kierkegaard's "little book" understands the Gospel text—"look to the birds of the air, consider the lily of the field"—on the basis of an imperative: *you shall* regard the lily and the bird as teachers in the essential; *you shall* learn from the lily and the bird to become silent. The meaning and origin of this imperative will have to be considered carefully. Initially, though, the imperative serves to mark a distinction between two antithetical modes of looking, that is, of relating to the phenomena of lily-bird-being. The one Kierkegaard calls "the poet" has a certain way of attending to the phenomena of the lily and the bird, a way ultimately to be rejected as an evasion; the gospel text demands another way of attending to the phenomena.

In these discourses "the poet" refers to a distinctive way of being, conceived on the basis of a certain attunement toward things and, more particularly, toward language. At the basis of the poet's self-understanding is the idea—central to both philosophical and biblical traditions—that the human "advantage," that is, its ontological distinctiveness, consists in language. The human being is the being with language. Poet existence, however, is permeated by pain (*Smerte*) precisely in relation to language: at the ground of the poet's existence, Kierkegaard indicates, is despair and melancholy. Why? The poet's existence takes root in—is enabled by and suffers from—the difference between poetic speech and "general" (*almindelige*) speech. In this difference the poet experiences nothing contingent, but a "brutal" loss: the irremediable loss of an original naïveté or immediacy in terms of which things appear in their original splendor, emergent out of the background of "solemnity." If the poet's existence is despair, it is because the poet inhabits that irreducible rift between the way things are given in general language and the way they may appear as emergent out of solemnity, which more precisely means: out of an essential *silence*.

Though the poet speaks, poetic attunement is organized wholly around silence as the background phenomenon. Indeed, "out there," where the lily and the bird are, the poet regards silence as the central phenomenon: "Out there is silence—and not just when all becomes silent in the silent night, but also during the day ... when everything is like an ocean of sound."[2] Nature maintains an essential silence in its totality, in its very sounding: "the sounding of nature belongs to silence, increases it, and to that extent maintains a mysterious correspondence with silence."[3] The poet understands the attunement toward silence as the essential condition of a speech that would allow things to appear freed from normalized meanings. Poetic speech, precisely as speech, is thus wholly conditioned by silence: "the poet [does not] seek silence in order to become silent; rather, the reverse, in order to speak—as the poet speaks."[4] What, then, is a poem? In the terms already set forth, Kierkegaard's answer is precise: "The poet lets everything resonate in pain—and this resonating of pain is the poem ... the infinite resonating [of the pain] is in itself the poem."[5] The measure and content of poetic speech, therefore, is the quality of its resonance, whether the poem lets the ontological pain of lost immediacy sound forth. In letting pain resonate, however, the poet discovers what he takes to be his central task: "he loans word and speech to the lily and the bird."[6] The task of the poet is to himself become, through language, the locus in which the lily and the bird achieve their manifestation. In this, again, he exercises his ontological privilege as the being endowed with language.

Thus Kierkegaard's discourse begins by invoking the way of being of the poet, the basic modality by which the poet lets things appear, speaks things forth. The provenance and adequacy of this conception of the poet[7] matters less, however, than its function in the discourse: the poet indicates a possibility of "evasion" and "excuse." "The poet is the child of eternal, but lacks the seriousness of the eternal."[8] Poetic existence lacks seriousness. More exactly, there is something in the poet's relation to silence—and consequently in his relation to speech—that is not serious. The poet attends to silence only as the enabling condition of speech and consequently lets all things appear only within the horizon of language; and all things so appearing appear as emblems of the essential loss the human being undergoes as a result of speech. The poet's discourse is tragic incantation.

The poet appears in these discourses, however, only to be set aside. The ultimate basis for this epoché of the poetic, Kierkegaard says, is that poetic attunement lacks seriousness and thus constitutes a form of evasion. But how? Evasion is founded upon and developed by the poet's initial relation to silence: the poet "reverses the relation" by making silence the condition of speech, whereas the attunement which attends towards the real, the serious relation, takes silence as the condition for becoming silent. As will be seen, the attunement presupposed in the Gospel text calls for an extraordinary movement "backwards" toward an origin prior to speech and not serving as the condition for speech. "In silence is the beginning" (*i Tavsheden er Begyndelsen*).[9] The poet's lack of seriousness, therefore, has its radical basis in a fundamental displacement and occlusion of the origin, which cannot be encountered in the resonance of the poem. It can be encountered in the lily and the bird, in learning silence from the lily and the bird.

The imperative

Proper attunement to lily-bird-being is to become silent, not as a condition for speech, but for becoming silent. However, the human being, as the living being with language, has the ontological "advantage" of speech—for Kierkegaard, a highly ambiguous advantage. Yet if silence is recognized more primordially than speech, if the human being is to learn the essential from the lily and the bird, who exist without speech, is this to suggest a critique of the fundamental determination of the human being as the being with language? Nevertheless speech always already permeates and normalizes human reality in the form of "general" speech. Keeping silence, therefore, will mean engaging the capability to speak in a new way: *either* the poet's way, where silence becomes the condition of speech, *or* the Gospel's way, where silence becomes the condition of silence. But for a being who is always already determined by speech, keeping silence is an *art*: "precisely because the human being can speak, precisely therefore it is an art to be able to keep silent; and just because his advantage so easily tempts him [to speech], therefore it is a great art to be able to keep silence."[10] What this art of keeping silence is shall have to be considered.

However, Kierkegaard marks a sharp distinction between poetic attunement and the art of becoming silent. It is a question of a different orientation toward "the beginning:" the poet seeks to draw forth the origin, the background solemnity in which all things resonate, into speech and so draw forth all beings—the lily, the bird—as though sprung out of this background. The poet's self-consciousness becomes the very locus in which the origin resonates. The poet is ultimately identical with his poem inasmuch as the poem *is* the resonance of the poet's pain, the poet's interiority. To this extent, the poet's "principle" is interiority, understood in terms of self-consciousness. The poet finds in self-consciousness a locus of being, the very foundation of the real. Kierkegaard's discourse hinges on a critique of poetic attunement and a critique of its foundation in self-consciousness. The poet is himself, one might say, the bloom of the modern foundation in self-consciousness, the flowering of the metaphysics of representation. The poet thinks to have realized in his poem an ontological function: to have become the very site in which the lily and the bird can resound, that is, manifest themselves out of the background silence, liberated from everyday speech. The poet frees the phenomena to be phenomena by his becoming silent. The poet discovers and relates to the origin of phenomenalization—indeed, identifies himself with this origin—in his own becoming silent he speaks origin-words.

Kierkegaard's critique of the poet is that, in its totality, the attunement lacks seriousness. But, again, where is the seriousness lacking? On the one hand, the poet trades in "the wish," that is, laments the forever-lost immediacy of being. The lily and the bird become tragic emblems over which he grieves. On the other hand the poet, knowing himself as the living being with speech, cannot take the lily and the bird as teachers in the essential because he regards their silence as a mere contingency of their being. They exist "without" speech, as a simple negation. Since the human being is the being with language, therefore, any effort to take the lily and the bird as the measure of the human cannot be serious—it can only be a matter of humor.

Against this whole poetic comportment Kierkegaard finds in the Gospel text an imperative: "you *shall* be as a bird," you shall learn silence from the lily and the bird. What is the meaning of this imperative? It is not simply a matter of raising biblical authority over poetic existence, for it would difficult to find, on purely grammatical grounds, an imperative as such in the biblical text. The imperative is to be understood rather in relation to the inner logic of the discourse itself. And, though the establishment of an imperative inevitably raises the specter of Kant's effort to ground morality in an unconditional imperative—at which point, analogously, Kant thought human life became serious—the imperative in this discourse has a completely different function. In particular, it is an imperative set forth—in sharp distinction from Kant's—without any prior grounding.

To hear the imperative appropriately "one must become a child again," and this in the precise sense that the "child does not inquire after grounds." The child's relation to the imperative is unmediated by a "laying of the foundations" (*Grundlegung*).[11] The child assents to the imperative without "deliberating" upon it, but takes it as immediately disclosive of a capability and a task: "Just because the child dare not say 'I can not,' neither is it true that he can not;

therefore it becomes apparent that he can; for it is impossible not to be able when one does not dare do otherwise; nothing is more certain."[12] There is a basic reversal articulated here: the child comes to understand himself, his capability, starting from the imperative. For the poet it is the other way around, he "reverses the relation:" he understands the imperative starting from his capability for speech—and thus does not take it seriously.

In the Gospel text, then, the imperative achieves absolute precedence. And this means more precisely: it functions to displace what the poet takes as the foundational reality, that is, self-consciousness. The lily and the bird exist without self-consciousness, without language, without the basic capability to represent themselves to themselves: in the imperative, lily-bird-being, precisely as such, is abruptly taken as the measure of the human. It is a measure adopted without the prior movement of grounding. Thus the function of the imperative in this discourse has nothing to do with any "moral" meaning; it has a primarily ontological significance. This latter is in fact the whole basis of its seriousness. The seriousness means: lily-bird-being, and not self-consciousness, is taken as the site to work out the problem of being as such. Nothing less than the question of being is at stake in the lily and the bird. How the lily and the bird realize a relation to being is taken as the measure of the human. The poet's lack of seriousness, then, is ultimately a failure to raise the question of being apart from the modern foundation in self-consciousness. The imperative intends an abrupt displacement of that foundation.

The beginning prior to speech

In contrast to the human being who exists on the basis of and as always already determined by speech, the lily and the bird maintain an essential silence. Silence is no mere negation, no mere lack in their being, but the terms in which their very being happens. Silence, then, is another name for being; to take the lily and the bird seriously as teachers in silence is to take silence seriously in its relation to being. Yet in these discourses comprising *The Lily of the Field and the Bird of the Air* Kierkegaard develops a rich problematic of being. To encounter silence is to encounter being according to one of its essential traits: the power of inception, the beginning. "In this silence," Kierkegaard writes, "is the beginning."[13] As such, silence is also internally connected to the event of temporalization, what Kierkegaard calls "the instant" (*Øieblikket*): "The instant only *is* in silence."[14] Being happens, with "no tidings to announce its arrival," in the sudden. And silence too involves an essential bond with suffering inasmuch as to be is to undergo being, to suffer being: "The bird is silent and suffers." To learn from the lily and the bird is to learn a certain attunement toward suffering, toward temporalization, and toward the way that being happens, an attunement attuned to silence. Yet, as shall be seen, becoming silent in no way signifies a mere absence of speech. It is a question—*an art*—of finding a language—and a comportment toward language—that deepens one's involvement in silence.

If speech is an "ambiguous advantage" it is because human beings exist initially as immersed in the "usual" speech, that is, exist in a world already determined in its totality by normalized meanings. Normalized meanings are incapable of making things determinate, a rift that becomes fully transparent in suffering. Though facing opposite directions, both the poet and the Gospel text alike thus involve, on the basis of a renewed relation to silence, a critique of *almindelige Tale*, that is, generalized speech. For the Gospel text, however, the prior determination of human reality by normalized meanings signifies that silence can be encountered only in a "backwards" direction, as having always already been occluded. Thus Kierkegaard writes: "In a definite way ... one comes backwards to the beginning. The beginning is not that with which one begins, but that at which one arrives; and one comes to it backwards."[15] It will be necessary to acknowledge an essential split between "the beginning with which one (normally) begins"—beginnings occurring on the basis of a world already determined in its totality by speech—and the beginning one can only arrive at through a backward movement of retreat—the inception of being itself. The backward movement, corresponding to the movement of becoming silent, encounters the beginning in an instant *prior to* the emergence of the normalized world.

The movement back to the beginning, to the instant of the incipience of speech itself—an instant *before* speech—is however an extraordinary movement. Kierkegaard clarifies it by commenting upon the Gospel text: "Seek first the Kingdom of God and his righteousness." He writes:

> But what does this mean, what I am supposed to do, or what kind of striving can be said to seek or pursue God's Kingdom? Shall I try to get a position corresponding to my abilities and powers in order to work in it? No, you shall seek *first* God's Kingdom. Shall I give my entire fortune to the poor? No, you shall seek *first* God's Kingdom ... So, in a certain sense there is nothing I should do? Yes, quite certainly, in a definite sense there is nothing [to do]. In the deepest sense you shall annihilate yourself (*gjøre dig selv til Intet*).[16]

The "Kingdom of God" would be in itself what is "first," that is, most originary; it would be another way of speaking about the instant of inception. To seek the originary "first" is not to undertake some first thing on a list of projects, but to establish a relation to the beginning, the instant of inception itself. Kierkegaard repeatedly draws a sharp line between such "originary" seeking and any possible project: "Is it *this* that I shall do, and when I do that is *that* what it means to seek God's Kingdom? The answer to that must be: No."[17] *Always No*. In relation to such seeking, there is absolutely nothing to do except put oneself in relation to the nothing that precedes speech, that is, become silent. The basis for this proscription on doing is clear: acting, casting oneself into the project, inaugurating a beginning within a world already constituted by normalized possibilities—that is, by speech—all these are essentially derivative modes, belated with respect to the beginning to which one can only arrive. Any possible project would be too late. To seek *first* is to establish a relation to that through which the spoken world is itself possible, to arrive back at the beginning that precedes speech, that precedes the horizon of the project.

The retreat to the beginning prior to speech, prior to the emergence of the normalized world, presupposes and is carried out through a movement of self-annihilation, of becoming nothing. Certainly it is a matter of becoming silent, but now Kierkegaard moves to give silence another expression. As indicated, silence does not mean the simple absence of speech. Kierkegaard says of silence of the bird, the example: "its silence is [in itself] a speaking" (*dens Tavshed er talende*). To seek first, to become silent, to retreat to the inceptive instant prior to speech: none of these are modes of the mere cessation of speech. They indicate rather a transformation in the relation to the human capability of speech: namely, an epoché of the sort of speech whose basic function is to represent things, to project future possibility, to arrange the world under "general" notions.

What speaking means apart from this still requires clarification. To anticipate, however: the silence that is in itself a speaking, would this not coincide with a *pure affirmation*, that is, an affirmation without conditions, and thus absolutely "first?" The bird's whole comportment is purely affirmative, that is, pure speaking. Speaking is here identical with being: the lily and the bird *are* the speaking. The "Kingdom of God," what is being thought here? Another name for the beginning, not from which one begins, but to which one arrives—the inceptive instant itself. Would not "the Kingdom of God" be reality as related to through pure affirmation? An attunement purely affirmative, whose affirmation occurs "before" anything to be affirmed, would not this indicate another kind of speaking than what takes place either in poetic speech or "usual" speech? These issues become decisive in the context of suffering.

Yet Kierkegaard is clear about what is lost in an attunement adopted wholly toward the spoken world and thus wholly toward the project: what is lost is an encounter with the instant itself, that is, with the inception of time that would be "pregnant with significance." The instant cannot, in principle, be encountered within a horizon determined by speech, but only in the attunement that withholds speech. Kierkegaard asks: "But wouldn't it still be possible to encounter 'the instant' while one is speaking? No: one only encounters the instant by becoming silent; insofar as one speaks, even if it is to say only a word, one misses the instant; the instant only *is* in silence."[18] This articulates a categorial exclusion whose basis must be clarified: the instant has no effective reality at all when brought within the horizon of speech; it cannot appear or be "encountered" (*træffet*). Given the way human life is always already cast within speech, this indicates the in-principle possibility of never encountering the instant: "Everything depends upon the instant; yet it is without doubt the great tragedy in the vast majority of people's lives, that they have never encountered the instant."[19] The condition for encountering the instant is becoming silent, the movement backwards toward the origin prior to speech.

The instant

Kierkegaard's discourse outlines the ontological stakes of silence in a categorial way: "the instant only *is* in silence." The instant: of itself "pregnant with significance," names the inceptive event of reality itself, the beginning prior to any beginning inaugurated within a present. The instant occurs prior to all present. The essential condition for encountering the instant—for a being who is determined by speech and the project—is to become *silent and wait* (*tier og bier*). The being of the lily and the bird consist in a silent waiting, an essential readiness. Readiness is not taken up as a particular attitude; rather, being-at-the-ready constitutes the whole being of lily-bird-being, and only in this way are they teachers. It is a matter of seriousness that, except on condition of this silent waiting, the instant cannot "appear," that is, cannot achieve its effective reality. It is entirely possible, even usual, to "let the instant slip by"[20] even though "everything depends on the instant." The critical questions, however, are these: how to account for the extreme phenomenological fragility of the instant; and then, how to clarify that in speech, or that modality of speaking, which occludes the instant as a matter of essence; and finally, why does silence allow the instant its effective reality?

Of itself, the instant is neither meaningful nor non-meaningful; it does not coincide with the happening of an event of great significance, whose terms could only be pre-delineated in a world already determined by speech. Kierkegaard is precise: the instant is "*pregnant* with rich significance." The instant is that whereby existence becomes fertile with possibility; it coincides, not with meaning as such—or with non-meaning—but with the inception of meaning. Thus one must learn how to "make use of the instant"[21] (*benytter Øieblikket*). The phenomenological fragility of the instant, that about it that demands silence and waiting, consists in the way it occurs: "it arrives with the light step of the sudden." Kierkegaard continues: "For the instant, even though pregnant with its rich significance, sends forth no messengers from itself to announce its arrival; it comes too quickly for that. When it comes, it is preceded by no instant of time."[22] Kierkegaard has formulated the way the instant happens here very carefully: it occurs "suddenly," that is, before there is time to form an anticipative horizon in which it could be received. In other words, the instant does not occur as an event *in* time—for example within the horizon of the temporal ecstasies of past-present-future—but as an "event" (this word is now problematic) that allows time, that inaugurates time. The being of the lily and the bird consists in proximity to this instant in which meaning has its inception: convinced that "everything happens in its time," they are silent and wait.

From its character as sudden it is possible to understand more clearly why the "instant only *is* in silence." Speaking—at least that speaking that occludes the instant—consists in establishing a relation with meaning, in projecting possibility, in the formation of a temporal horizon, and in the preparation of a receptivity that already maintains a relation with what is to be received. To speak in this way is to thus exist within a horizon in which projects can be initiated, projects whose possibility already exists and call to one. Yet existence oriented in this way essentially misses the instant. The instant cannot, in principle, be encountered within an already prepared horizon of meaning. It is not an event that has its inception within a meaningful horizon and plays out along that horizon. The instant has no duration: it arrives suddenly, "without sending any messengers before itself" to announce its arrival: in other words, it comes without having prepared the ground for itself, without awakening the anticipatory structures by which it may be properly received. It arrives "without having been preceded by an instant of time," that is, it does not double itself up and allow the slenderest of anticipations. It arrives when it arrives. In relation to the instant, therefore, the only thing one can do—this is what the lily and the bird do—is wait and maintain silence. A waiting silence constitutes the essential condition in which one can sense (*fornemme*) that "now it is here"—"and in the next moment, it is gone."

Thus the sudden temporality of the instant, which is discontinuous, is exclusive of the durational temporality in which meaning is allowed to gather and projects to be formed. It is owing to this that the instant involves a relation to the "eternal." The eternal and the sudden say the same thing: the instant does not occur within, but breaks in upon, an already constituted temporal horizon. Here again it is necessary to distinguish the beginning to which one can only arrive in a backward movement—the inceptive instant itself—and any beginning inaugurated in a present. The instant has its beginning, as it were, in the eternal—which means prior to any temporal horizon in which it can be anticipated. The instant bears eternity within itself insofar as it arrives when it arrives, preceded by nothing, not even itself.

Even though "pregnant with significance," the instant cannot be thought of in terms of meaning, as if it coincided with a meaningful event. The instant is neither meaningful nor meaningless. Rather, it is that wherein meaning has its inception and so always, and essentially, occurrent *just prior* to meaning, at the cusp of meaning, so to speak. The *pregnancy* of the instant is its decisive mode: the event of birth, even though anticipated, exceeds the structures of anticipation. Birth is surprise, the unprecedented. The instant, rather than being incorporated into an already meaningful temporal horizon, shatters this with the unprecedented. Yet the unprecedented can be related to as the unprecedented, the instant as instant, only on condition of silence: which is to say, only on condition of a *fundamental reticence* to ascribe meaning to what one is undergoing. The turning back toward meaning is the return to language and representation.

The lily and the bird, consequently, are silent in their absolute reticence to ascribe meaning. Rather than speaking, rather than anticipating what reality will have meant, they wait. Silence is in itself a waiting, an essential waiting that is not a waiting-for something anticipated: "the bird is silent and waits; it knows...that everything will occur in its season, hence the bird waits." To maintain silence is to let reality be the criterion of itself, to let it unfold as it will unfold, and to attune oneself to this. To maintain silence is to abandon the anticipative nets by which we capture a reality that unfolds through its own accord.

The nature of this reticence to ascribe meaning can be understood, however, only through its antithesis to speech and to the project. Inasmuch as they are silent and wait, the lily and the bird exist without project. Projects have their foundation in the anticipation of meaning and thus in a relation to the future insofar as the future announces itself prior to its arrival. The instant arrives before announcing itself. In principle, then, there can be no project directed toward the instant, nor any project founded upon the instant. Indeed, the attempt to anticipate the instant prior to its arrival, so as to inaugurate some project in relation to it, is exactly what constitutes the speech in which the instant is occluded. Speaking and projecting wholly coincide. The instant only *is* in silence; it can only be encountered in a suspension of speaking-projecting. Nevertheless, when the instant arrives, it arrives as "the opportune time" (*den beleilige Tid*); it may be used. What then is "the making use of the instant," if not a project? Does not the instant give way to, and radically found, the project structure? What constitutes making use of the opportune time? As will be seen, it is a question of a relation to suffering, not the project; it concerns not a doing, but the how of an undergoing.

Suffering

Kierkegaard abruptly introduces suffering into this discourse as what seems like a new, contingent determination: "*The bird is silent and suffers.*"[23] In fact, suffering constitutes the innermost concern of the discourse and organizes its understanding of silence, language and temporalization (the instant). For the human being—the being with language—suffering is tied in a critical and essential way with speech: how to speak about suffering, how to express what one is undergoing, how to find a language? These are questions bearing centrally upon the poet too except that the poet—according to the conception Kierkegaard has developed—adopts an essentially tragic incantation, speaking of the rift underneath consciousness, the loss of immediacy, thus displacing suffering in the gladness of a poem. These are also questions bearing upon "general" speech: consolatory discourses of all kinds, metaphysically grounded or not, up to and including theodicies.

For the living being with language, it seems, the effort to make suffering *mean* something is irresistible. Although speech is and remains the human "advantage," it effectively becomes so only as it *becomes* silent. Only in a reticence to speak and to ascribe meaning does this advantage effectively realize itself. The lily and the bird are silent insofar as their comportment in suffering realizes itself in a fundamental reticence to make their suffering mean (or not mean) something. Such reticence, however, is not equivalent to the mere cessation of speech; it rather coincides with the paring down of speech to the determinate—or, otherwise put, the refusal to place suffering within a milieu of indeterminacy. The drift of language itself, however, is toward the indeterminate. Hence, silence becomes an art of speaking determinately. Kierkegaard writes:

> But why is it that, compared to the suffering of the lily, human suffering seems so anguished? Is it not just that the lily cannot speak? If the lily could speak ... if it hadn't learned the art of silence, perhaps then its suffering would be anguished. But the lily maintains silence. For the lily to suffer is to suffer, neither more nor less. Indeed, precisely when suffering is neither more nor less than suffering, the suffering is made as singular and uncomplicated (*enfoldig*) as is possible to make it ... Suffering cannot be made less, for it indeed *is*, and consequently is what it is ... When suffering is neither more nor less than it is, thus when suffering only is the determinate thing that it is, it is minimized to the extent it can be, even if it is the greatest suffering.[24]

Silence consists in forming a determinate relation to the determinate. In speech, this immediately takes tautological form: suffering is what it is, neither more nor less than suffering; *it is*. But the tautological language—which in itself has no content—brings suffering to determinacy only, indirectly, by its exclusion of indeterminate speech. The exclusion of indeterminate speech, however, raises the most essential and critical problem for the being with language: "But when suffering becomes indeterminate, however great it is, it becomes greater; such indetermination increases suffering infinitely. And such indetermination arises precisely through the human being's ambiguous advantage of having the capability of speech."[25]

Yet, what kind of speaking about suffering makes it indeterminate? Any speech that would conjure away that *suffering is*. Suffering is negated as suffering—meaning conjured away—whenever it is treated as a mere contingency, incidental to being. The silence of the lily and the bird consists in their immediate grasp of the identity of being and suffering being. This bond—where being is at once the suffering of being—constitutes what Kierkegaard calls the "simplicity" of suffering. To try to evade this bond, to step outside of it, to represent it, to make it mean something, is ultimately an effort to render it contingent and only to reproduce a new and exacerbated form of suffering. To minimize suffering, to become silent, is to allow it to be suffering—to allow it *to be* without an assigned meaning. This is an art closely related to "making use of the instant."

Making use of the instant

What occurs in the instant? Perhaps nothing. Only in silence is the instant effective. But that is to say: only in a certain attunement toward suffering, characterized by a fundamental reticence to ascribe to it meaning (or non-meaning), does the instant allow itself to be encountered and made use of: "When the instant comes the silent bird understands that it is the instant; it uses it and is never put to shame;" "then comes the instant and when the instant arrives the silent lily understands that now is the instant and it uses it."[26] What it is to use the instant? Using the instant: since it is not preceded by any anticipation, it cannot be a project. It arrives. Using the instant is not even a matter of receiving it. Implied in the idea of use is: *one uses it and lets it go*. Uses it for what? For the task of becoming silent, which ultimately means: losing one's name, losing one's ownmost interiority, losing one's projects. Losing the self. The instant is the enabling condition by which the self can lose itself. To use the instant is to let go a little bit more. This use of the instant is closely related to "obedience."

Discourse II: obedience

The three discourses that comprise *The Lily of the Field and the Bird of the Air* are organized around the development of the attunement developed in discourse 3: joy "over nothing," "unconditioned joy," "being joy itself." Or one could say, "pure affirmation." Itself without occasioning cause, the lily and the bird communicate joy through being it; their being *is* their communication and joy is communicative of itself. On the part of the human being who would learn such joy, however, some initial conditions are presupposed. Learning joy, realizing joy, involves the preparatory attunements of silence (discourse 1) and obedience (discourse 2). Silence and obedience together constitutes the inner conditions, on the side of the learner, for "being joy itself" (*Glæden selv*).

As indicated, at stake in silence is a reticence to ascribe meaning to what one is undergoing. Silence is a withholding of the basic gesture of speech: the inscription of all things within a horizon of generalized meanings. And the silence of the lily and the bird goes further: it refuses the deepening gesture of poetic speech, which draws things—not from the general sense—but from their background in solemnity; it sees things in the mystery of their emergence. The silence of the lily and the bird is born in suffering: concerning suffering speech is reduced to tautology, "to suffer is to suffer." Casting suffering within a generalized horizon, poetic or not, is an effort to make suffering *not* be; but suffering *is*. So silence is letting suffering be suffering, without the ascription of meaning (or non-meaning). Learning this silence, Kierkegaard says, it is "the first condition for really being able to obey." Obedience, as an attunement, is another modality of silence, a deepening of silence.

Clarifying the meaning of obedience in these discourses requires care, however.[27] Kierkegaard's initial articulation of obedience frames it ontotheologically: obedience describes the relation between the creator and the created as one constituted by a necessity grounded in the "almighty" will of God: "and because God is the Almighty, therefore nothing happens, not even the least thing, without his will." The divine will, itself unconditioned, conditions every event, every sparrow falling to the ground." "In nature all is unconditioned obedience." Nature in its totality is "the conditioned"—which means, the created—God's will, no different than God's being, is the unconditioned. Everything occurs according to necessity (*Nødvendighed*). Kierkegaard writes: "there is nothing else but God's unconditioned will; if there were not God's unconditioned will, at the very moment everything would cease to exist."[28] According to its first articulation, then, unconditioned obedience indicates the being of nature in its totality as subject to the divine will—created—and thereby to necessity. The human being too is included in this order of necessity: "You also are submitted to necessity."[29]

Though the discourse initially frames the issue of obedience using resources drawn from ontotheology—God's will as unconditioned being—in its development of this problematic it slips obliquely from this frame. The real problem of this discourse, the problem of obedience, is finding an attunement—learning it from the lily and the bird—in which one is properly attuned to necessity. The lily and the bird accomplish this without further ado. For the human being, who has to learn a relation to necessity, there is a "danger" to be run. Further, in the context of learning necessity, necessity takes on a wholly phenomenological character. In particular, the notion of necessity is understood neither in terms of efficient causal laws nor metaphysical-teleological finality; it is not understood, in other words, according to a "principle of sufficient reason" and it does not operate in the discourse to provide grounding for a total conception, for a total meaning.

The contrary is the case: necessity, according to its phenomenological figure, refers to the *being-emplaced* of all beings within a site in excess to one's power to determine. Necessity refers first of all to the being-always-already-given of a being within a determinate "place," in conditions that one can nevertheless not determine. The totality of nature, inclusive of the human being, always already finds itself emplaced, within a determinate context (*Omgivelse*), that it did not determine through its own agency. Necessity is encountered as that force which is always already operative as emplacing and as the very indeterminability of the place one finds oneself. Encountering the necessity of being-emplaced, the human being makes an effort to inhabit that place. This work of inhabiting place, Kierkegaard says, takes shape as the fundamental project of "determining the place and the condition," that is, appropriating the place. Preceded by any such project however, is the deeper work of *obedience*: "Only by means of unconditional obedience can one unconditionally accurately encounter 'the place' where one can stand."[30] Consequently, obedience is first about finding place and finding oneself emplaced: within the indeterminable excess of being-emplaced, it concerns hitting upon the place where one is able to find ground under one's feet, a place to stand. Obedience concerns therefore the most originary relation to place, that is, to the event of one's being-emplaced. It is not a mere submission to place, but the modality by which one assumes place. The event of one's being-emplaced also involves a temporality—the instant—and so obedience involves an originary relation to temporalization: "only unconditioned obedience can unconditionally accurately encounter 'the instant.'"[31] So obedience, as an attunement, concerns the most originary relation to space-time that a being can assume; it implies concourse with the origin, the beginning prior to the beginning. As is evident, obedience in this sense has nothing to do with any moral problematic; it is rather of an ontological order. The lily and the bird, as the very mode of their unconditioned obedience, dwell wholly in the event of spatialization-temporalization, at the incipience of being itself; a human being, however, must learn that in the encounter with necessity and in running a certain "danger."

Necessity and whylessness

Obedience is a relation to necessity; and necessity, in its first articulation, concerns the being-emplaced of all things within a context is always-already given, apart from a being's power to determine it, and hence one that escapes determination. Necessity, however, bears down even more intimately upon the beings so situated, in a way that brings time-space together: the sharpest articulation of necessity concerns the essential jointure, affecting the being of every being, of "becoming and destruction" (*Tilblivelse og Undergang*). Being subject to necessity means existing in the inescapability of this jointure wherein coming-to-be—for example, the blooming of the lily—and destruction "are one." For the lily, its whole instant, the very event of its being, is dominated by this jointure; *so too the human*, where lily-being is taken as the measure of human being. The notion of necessity in this context takes on the concrete figure of *whylessness*: "it even seems that [the lily] came into to being and became glorious [only] *so that* it could undergo destruction."[32] Necessity thus presses down as the whylessnesss of becoming. A becoming inwardly oriented toward, and so dominated, by destruction—rather than by the realization of an anticipated end-goal—is without reason, that is, without principle or end-goal. Yet, for a being wholly conditioned by the unconditioned, this is how being unfolds. If one imagines a human being in face of such an event—that is, *thinks the actual situation of the human*—in place of the lily, Kierkegaard says, he would presumably respond by seeking a why: " 'For what purpose?' he would say . . . 'why?' . . . 'what is the use?' "[33] The very idea of a becoming that is inwardly determined, claimed in advance by death, such that coming-to-be and death belong essentially together, subjects being to the absence of why in the most fundamental way. And *this* is the context in which obedience, as an attunement and a task to be learned, takes on its concrete meaning: the concrete occurrence of being is stripped of principle or end-goal, in such a way that becoming and destruction "are one." Being subject to necessity is being subject to this anarchy. It is enough to bring a human being to despair: "We human beings, in place of the lily, would perhaps despair over the thought that coming-into-being and destruction were one thing; and that despair would hinder us from becoming what we could have become, if only for an instant."[34] It is then a question of unconditional obedience *or* despair. Here we approach "the danger."

The lily, however, is emblematic in fully realizing unconditioned obedience: that is, in fully immersing itself in the "instant" in which its blooming and its destruction are one thing. This in fact constitutes precisely the *glory* (*Deiligheden*) of the lily: the lily was "unconditionally obedient, therefore it became itself in all its glory, it actually became its entire possibility (*hele sin*

Mulighed), undisturbed, unconditionally undisturbed by the thought that the same moment was its death."[35] Only unconditioned obedience is capable of investing the living being with "the faith and courage to become in all its glory," to realize its entire possibility, if only for an instant. Unconditioned obedience, presupposing the essential jointure of becoming and death, grants the wherewithal to bloom, to become one's entire possibility, fully to inhabit and to bloom in that finite, an-archic time-space.

Being unconditionally obedient signifies becoming *finite without restriction*, becoming "one's entire possibility, if only for a moment." Needless to say, becoming finite without restriction is not a project, but the ever-renewed effort to be: "the obedient bird begins the work [of finding the attunement of obedience] all over again, each day, with the same effort and care as the first time ... unconditionally undisturbed by the next instant."[36] Acting without end-goal, without project, without a why: unconditioned obedience in which there is no "next instant."

Love and hate

The objection, however, is ever present: "For the lily and the bird it is easy to be obedient; they cannot do otherwise." The unconditioned obedience of the lily and the bird is woven into the pattern of being itself: it is not a *doing* in the fullest sense. For the human being, however, achieving a relation to necessity does not follow of itself—it is a matter of a choice, a fundamental *either-or*: "*Either* love God *or* hate him." But this will be to say: either love necessity or hate it, either unconditioned obedience or, or what? Necessity remains necessity, so in reality there is no "or" in this either-or: "There is an either/or: either *God*— or, yes, the rest is indifferent ... Therefore: either *God.*"[37] The human being, confronting necessity, confronts a fundamental choice in which there is only one thing to choose. God, or necessity, plays a double role here. God is not merely an object of choice—for example, a being chosen in preference to other beings—but simultaneously what posits the choice as a choice: "it is actually God himself, being the object of choice, who intensifies the decisiveness of the choice, so that it really becomes an either/or."[38] God is what is chosen and the condition of the possibility of choosing it. This is to say that the confrontation with God, or necessity, is the one inexorable thing, the "danger" the human being must face: "This monstrous danger, that 'the human being' is placed between these two monstrous powers and given over to the choice that makes it so that one must either love or hate, and that not to love is to hate."[39]

The true human position—in distinction from the lily and the bird—is to be placed in the danger of this *choice*: either love, that is, unconditional obedience, or hate, that is, despair and resentment. It is an absolute choice in the sense that what is at stake is one's attunement, not toward this or that thing, but toward being as such. It is a choice about comporting oneself with *how reality happens*, rather than what happens. Reality occurs with necessity, determining all beings within an indeterminable context, subjecting all beings to the essential jointure of becoming and destruction, and hence exposing all beings to a fundamental whylessness. The choice is: love this, or. Unconditioned obedience is to love being as being; it is a modality of affirmation. It is really affirmation. To really affirm reality in its necessity, however, it is not enough to *recognize* the necessity of affirmation—that is, to grasp that there really is only one choice. It is not enough "that a human being first understands that it is so and thereupon resolves to unconditionally obey."[40] One doesn't come to affirmation by mere recognition of the character of being—recognizing, for example, the inescapability of necessity. Unconditioned obedience, in other words, is not conditioned by a prior act of understanding. Rather, it is the other way around: "by means of unconditioned obedience does a human being first come to understand."[41] Only in the act of affirming without any conditions does it become possible to understand the necessity of affirming and the monstrous danger of not affirming. Love-affirmation-obedience: these constitute what is "first," a practical a priori, within whose attunement the human being—as the lily and the bird—becomes absolutely *pliant to being in its happening*.

It is the attunement in which the human being finds time-space in which to "become all its possibility, if only for a moment."

The auto-didacticism of obedience

Unconditioned obedience cannot, strictly speaking, be commanded—nor even taught. And this in spite of the fact that, according to Kierkegaard, the lily and the bird do teach and the Gospel commands that the human being should learn it. It cannot strictly speaking be taught owing to its nature as what necessarily comes before the act of recognition and understanding. It is a distortion, Kierkegaard has said, to imagine that one must first hear unconditioned obedience commanded, or first encounter it in the lily and the bird, and then resolve to accomplish it. No free resolution precedes or conditions unconditioned obedience. Rather, unconditioned obedience is learned and recognized only in unconditioned obedience: it is in every way the inceptive act. Of the lily and the bird Kierkegaard writes: "What is that wherein he teaches obedience? In obedience. And by means of what does he teach obedience? By means of obedience. If you could become obedient like the lily and the bird then you also would be able to learn obedience *from yourself*."[42] This is obedience's practical a priori: obedience is learned only in becoming obedient, that is, out of the nature of the human being's relation with being, in attunement to that, and not out of any external teaching or command. This is the fundamental auto-didacticism of obedience such that it coincides, not with submission and heteronomy, but with a blooming of unrestricted finitude.

Discourse III: joy itself

Each of the three discourses—on silence, obedience and joy—clarifies a modality of unconditioned life. Silence and obedience, however, are nothing separate from joy, but constitute its inner conditions: so much silence and obedience, so much joy. This will alter, in an essential way, what is meant by an "unconditioned" life.

The lily and the bird realize in their being, as the way of the being, a life liberated from all conditions: a life of "unconditioned joy." This does *not* mean, however, a life liberated from finitude. As becomes clear in the third discourse, the being of the lily and the bird is at the same time inwardly constituted by an "infinite sorrow" (*uendelig Sorg*). Kierkegaard invokes the Pauline theme that the totality of creation is subject to "corruption," the sigh of the creature. To the extent that the lily and the bird—just as the human being—are *subject* to being, that is, find themselves given over to being, inextricably involved in it with no exit, they suffer ontological "imprisonment." An unconditioned life, far from being a liberation from this condition, in fact presupposes it. The lily and the bird, "though they carry an infinitely deep sorrow, yet are unconditionally joyful and are joy itself."[43] An unconditioned life is thus constituted by the simultaneity of infinite sorrow and unconditioned joy. To this corresponds a unique comportment that Kierkegaard names, in a term difficult to translate, "*Eftergivenhed*."[44] The term indicates a suppleness or pliancy, a capacity to receive. Leather, for example, has this quality in its capacity to receive etchings and inscriptions. An earlier tradition, Eckhartian in provenance, would perhaps name this comportment *Gelassenheit*. What is at stake is a stance towards reality that actively lets reality be the criterion of itself, which "lets things be," something that presupposes silence and obedience.

To speak of an unconditioned life is not to speak of life on the basis of an unconditioned ground, secured in advance by thought, but life as the expression of a prior attunement to being as such—that is, to the beginning that always precedes one, to the pre-originary origin. Silence and obedience—and in the third discourse, joy—each constitute a relation with the inception of being; each hit upon "the instant" with accuracy. Silence and obedience are attunements that allow one to find time and place, to inhabit one's site, to become one's "entire possibility, if even for a moment." As attunements, silence and obedience constitute the inner conditions for a joy that is without conditions: the lily and the bird "are unconditionally joyful, are joy itself." Liberated from any condition, their joy—their being joyful—is groundless, it is a joy "over nothing at all"[45] (*slet Intet*). Yet this "over nothing at all" is another way of speaking about being as such: the lily and the bird take joy in being as being, apart from any conditions. Even more, they do not merely take joy in being, they realize and express being as joy; they are "joy itself." Joy is here not merely one "emotion" among others— for example, the most important emotion—but rather identifies the milieu in which being communicates itself, expresses itself, becomes available: that is, the way being becomes existence. To exist is to *express* being, to "use the instant," to give concrete shape to the relation to the unconditioned.

If in silence, obedience and joy, then, Kierkegaard names a relation to the unconditioned—and thus clarifies the modalities of an unconditioned life—this must be understood more exactly. As indicated, it is not a question of securing the unconditioned in advance as the basis upon which to live. This could not be the case insofar as it would locate access to the unconditioned in some prior condition: in a beginning inaugurated in the present, as an act of thought or representation, whereas the unconditioned precedes any such beginning. To live in the unconditioned is to strike a relation, not to what becomes available in presence, but to the inception of presence. For this reason the attunements of silence, obedience and joy have an essentially a priori dimension: not conditioned by any present, not tied to any particular event, they are *carried into* every event. Joy, for example, is not founded upon anything; it is rather *founding*, in the sense that it establishes the condition, prior to the present, within which the present is lived or "used." In being-joy, without condition, each moment is lived as joy.

Being as presence

The lily and the bird, being joy itself, necessarily communicate joy. To be is to communicate being, to express being. But, Kierkegaard asks, what do the lily and the bird communicate in communicating being-as-joy? Does joy have any content, can it be clarified conceptually in terms of its "thought determinations?" The lily and the bird, Kierkegaard says, are "certainly not thoughtless." Their being is constituted, not as bare presence, but as an "acquired originariness." The being of the lily and the bird is, from the beginning, in an explicit relation to the origin. This does not mean that the lily and the bird think or represent the origin to themselves, or exist on the basis of self-consciousness, but only that their being has an intelligibility to it that can be communicated and clarified. If the lily and the bird are not thoughtless, if they "think," this is also to say that they *speak*—not, however, as a function of having language as a representational power, but as a function of their being itself. Their being *is* their logos; they are themselves what they communicate. And what they communicate is being itself, what it means to be.

What, then, is this logos of the lily and the bird? Kierkegaard summarizes: "their instruction in joy, which again their lives express, is ... this: 'there is a today; there *is*'. An infinite emphasis falls upon this *is*. 'There is a today,' and there is no concern at all for tomorrow." An infinite emphasis falls upon the "is" in "there is a today."[46] Given this, one could say that lily and the bird express *that there is being*, that *being is*. The very being of the lily and the bird consists in a bringing the thought of being—the "is" in "there is a today"—to a point of infinite intensity. In their being, that is, the lily and the bird bring being to presence; and being-brought-to-presence is "joy itself," the inception of "today." Their whole being plays out at the cusp of being, as it were, which is to say at its inception, in the instant itself, which occurs always prior to the time inaugurating by self-consciousness.

The lily and the bird, in bringing being to its intensification and communicability, bring being to its clearest thought determination: being signifies joy. To be *is* to realize and express joy—not as a function of some particular act or emotion, but as the way of being itself. The lily and the bird *are* "joy itself" and hence expressive of joy. Joy is at once what constitutes their being and what expresses it. Nothing is said about whether they feel joy; indeed, a strict distinction should be made between joy as a particular emotion, for example, and joy as a way the lily and the bird relate to their being. Joy is *how* being is: both that in which being comes to presence and that which is communicated in its coming to presence. Joy, however, can be further determined according to its concept. "What is joy," Kierkegaard asks, "or what is it to be joyful?" Kierkegaard clarifies the "thought determinations" of joy in a series of traits. Joy is: 1) "to be present to oneself (*sig selv nærværende*); 2) "being today" (*at være i Dag*); 3) "the present time with the entire emphasis upon: *the present time (den nærværende Tid)*."[47] To think being as joy—or, conversely, to think joy as the very expression of being—is to think being as presence.

The nature of this presence, however, must be carefully determined. Joy is "the present time" but, Kierkegaard adds in a tautological repetition, "with the entire emphasis upon: *the present time*." Why the emphasis, the doubling? This coincides with the infinite emphasis put on "is" in "there *is* a today." It is not enough to say that joy grasps being as presence; rather, in joy—or as joy—being is thought as the emphasis, the intensification of presence. Joy is the very resonance of "is" in "there is a today." Joy is the *present coming to presence*, receiving emphasis as presence. In the present coming to presence, the self becomes present to itself. Joy is this coincidence whereby the coming-to-presence of being is, in the same instant, the coming-to-self-presence of the self to itself—literally, its *being-near-to* itself. Such self-proximity constitutes a definite mode of temporality: being today. In the intensification of being, only "today" is—"tomorrow" is not. And with the annihilation of tomorrow concern about tomorrow loses its basis.

Presupposed in unconditioned joy, therefore, is an account of being in which a certain mode of temporality—presence, "today,"—is privileged. However, essential questions arise in relation to this. Does not the interpretation of being as presence place Kierkegaard's account within those traditions identified as "metaphysical?" In other words, in the figure of unconditioned joy, has not Kierkegaard uncritically taken over the oldest "prejudice" of the philosophical tradition—namely, that the real is untouched by any "outside," any temporality or difference, any death or finitude? Even more sharply: in giving privilege, not only to the general figure of presence, but to *self-presence*, does not Kierkegaard repeat the fundamental gesture of the modern metaphysics of self-consciousness—namely, grasping the constant self-presence of the ego, its lack of any difference, in its capacity as a foundation? Is there no work of difference or delay already at work as the condition of the self?[48] In short: is unconditioned joy a pseudo or fantasmatic figure of life, an effort to conceive life as untouched by finitude, temporality, and mortality?

As has already been indicated, however, unconditioned joy somehow includes infinite sorrow; its context is the "corruptibility" of all things. Joy is not, therefore, a liberation from finitude. Nor is the self-presence that constitutes joy interpretable in terms of self-certainty of self-consciousness. Its presence to itself occurs, neither in its spontaneous positing of itself nor its pure grasp of itself—as in idealism—but only against the background of its "being confined, being bound, in prison." To be is to "have been subjected against [one's] will" to the unsurpassable ontological situation of being imprisoned-in-self. This fundamentally passive bond with self, the originary suffering, is the source of the "sigh" of the creature, its infinite sorrow. To be is to suffer being, to be subjected to being. Unconditioned joy therefore, far from being untouched by suffering, both presupposes and occurs simultaneous with it: "even though [the lily and the bird] bear such an infinitely deep sorrow, they nevertheless are unconditionally joyful and are joy itself."[49]

The simultaneity of joy and suffering decisively changes the meaning of self-presence in joy: to be present to oneself in the manner of joy includes assuming the condition of corruptibility. This is exactly why, as Kierkegaard underscores, joy emerges only on condition of the prior movements of silence and obedience. Silence and obedience accomplish the destruction of the modes of projected time and the meanings that are formed within that horizon, upon that basis. As indicated, they clear the way for an encounter with "the instant" and the "the place." They allow the originary event of giving time and allowing space to occur. This movement beyond the structures of projected time-space, back to the "beginning," coincides with the irruption of joy itself: "But when, on the basis of silence and obedience, tomorrow does not exist, then for this reason—in silence and obedience—this day today is—it *is*—and so joy is."[50] Today emerges in its presence only when tomorrow and yesterday have been bracketed out, set back into non-being.

What in fact comprises this "today?" What is included and excluded? What is *excluded* is "tomorrow and the day after tomorrow," that is, the future that arises on the basis of anticipative projection. In joy there is no ecstasis toward the future. Being self-present thus signifies *not* being-ahead-of-oneself in project. Nor, for the same reason, is there any "yesterday." In a note to the text Kierkegaard writes: "the difficulty is, namely, to have the day today without any presuppositions."[51] Having the day wholly without presupposition, however, can only signify that "today" is lived as a beginning from itself, or absolute beginning. "Today"—the present exclusive of tomorrow and yesterday—is consequently the temporality of a beginning that is not a beginning towards anything definite, that is, not the beginning of a project. "Today," being self-present, is *being-underway* simply. It is the instant of immersion in time-space when one *is* what one is doing and what one is doing *is* what one is. The blooming of the lily *is* the lily; the taking wing of the bird *is* the bird. Blooming, taking wing, is the finding time and place of the finite creature. That this blooming, for example, is always already captured by "corruptibility" rivets it to infinite sorrow, but changes nothing about the blooming itself. The blooming, for example, only becomes "pointless" on condition of stepping outside the event and reframing it within some horizon of meaning—representing the blooming with respect to some "yesterday" or "tomorrow." In silence and obedience blooming is simply blooming, nothing more and nothing less. Only today is.

"Today" therefore cannot be conflated with constant "now" of presence set off in relation to future and past. Nor can the self-presence of joy be conflated with the transcendental self-presence of the ego to itself, for example Fichte's self-positing "I." Fichte's I=I, which definitively promotes self-presence to the status of a ground, is presupposed in all idealisms, up to the present. What "today" signifies in the context of joy, however, is something different: it is in general not an a priori, constituting structure, not the "form of inner sense" as Kant understood time. "Today" is not that which *constitutes* the presence of the present; it is not, therefore, that which founds and guarantees meaning. Apart from all these, which treat self-presence as in itself an originary structure, Kierkegaard asserts the paradoxical figure of an originariness that one arrives at: an acquired originariness. Self-presence rather coincides with the always prior beginning related to in silence and obedience. Everything depends upon "today" having its prior condition in these backwards movements of silence and obedience: only silence and obedience encounter the instant, only silence and obedience allow one to assume space and to use time.

Eftergivenhed: *pliancy as radical attunement*

But what precise mode of attunement corresponds to being-today? Kierkegaard asks: "but how do the lily and the bird comport themselves ... it seems like a miracle: in the deepest sorrow to be unconditionally joyful. Where tomorrow is such a frightful thing, *to be*, that is, to be unconditionally joyful, how do they comport themselves?"[52] In other words, what is the actual mode of existing within the coincidence of infinite sorrow and unconditioned joy? How, presupposing infinite sorrow, do the lily and the bird actually enact this beginning that is not a beginning conceived as the present and consequently not a beginning of the project? How do they remain *at* the beginning? Kierkegaard draws from a biblical text to give initial framing to the comportment: "Cast *all* your sorrow upon God." Kierkegaard insists that the phrase be taken "literally." The infinite sorrow of corruptibility, lived as both being subject to mortality and whyless necessity, must be thrust away, displaced onto God. The literality of this expression concerns its being a *total* act, an act which defines the comportment the lily and the bird *bring with them* into each moment. The moment, the "today," never signifies anything other than joy precisely because the infinite sorrow has always already been "cast" onto God. Kierkegaard writes: "In the same now (*Nu*)—and this same now is today from the very first instant that it exists—in the same now the [lily and the bird are] unconditionally joyful."[53] The comportment within which "today" emerges, within which the presence undergoes infinite intensification, within which the bird and the lily become present to themselves in such a way that tomorrow and yesterday do not exist, is called by Kierkegaard "*Eftergivenhed*"[54]—a term which suggests a receptive pliancy, a capability of taking on inscriptions. The lily and the bird, through their silence and obedience, have jettisoned all notions about how reality is *supposed* to go; they have become pliant to the happening of reality itself, allowing reality to be the criterion of itself. In becoming wholly pliant to reality they take on *its* inscriptions, unmediated by any anticipative projects grounded in the recollection of the past. Thus "to cast one's cares," a term that might suggest the "deployment of force," in fact signifies the opposite: "to cast" is simply to *let-go* all notions about reality founded in the inaugural power of the ego. In this letting-go there is gathering (*Samling*) of the self to itself in presence; the self no longer lives ahead of itself in project or behind itself in recollection. It is also important that one cast one's care—Kierkegaard also says "literally,"—upon *God*. Casting them anywhere else constitutes mere dispersal (*Adspredelsen*). Why upon God, precisely? An infinite sorrow escapes schematization in terms of speech horizons. The attempt to invest it within meaningful context, therefore, only intensifies, not relieves it. While the poet may take this sorrow as the condition of the poem, silence and obedience understand it as the exigency to let-go absolutely: that is, to let go expecting nothing in return. The creature must become pliant, absolutely pliant, to what they're undergoing; must take the measure of reality and itself from what it is undergoing; and not attempt to gain mastery of the event by reframing it as a "moment" in a larger project. "God" is here is placeholder for the essence of reality as what escapes one's control, but also a placeholder for the affirmability of reality outside contexts of meaning. Reality can be affirmed without that affirmation being grounded in a meaning: that is precisely what *Eftergivenhed* accomplishes. The joy of the lily and the bird affirm reality in its totality without grounding that affirmation on any particular event or meaning. A groundless affirmation is in fact the only counter movement toward infinite sorrow. Infinite sorrow is never eradicated, since it constitutes the being of the creature, it is simply taken as itself something to affirm. Casting all one's sorrows "upon God," letting the infinite be infinite, does not eliminate this sorrow, but relativizes it with respect to the joy of the instant itself: that, despite all, time and place are ceded, that inhabitation of space and time *remain* as fundamental possibilities to be made use of.

Postscript: the edifying and the tragic

The edifying discourse has lately come under suspicion, in particular, in the context of the critique of metaphysics, that is, of thinking organized around the attempt to secure for human life some normative foundation. The very concept of edification—that is, building up—seems to invoke a foundational discourse: if one is to build well, one can only build on a foundation. In this regard it is perhaps necessary to ask: to what extent is it the case that the edifying discourse has, as its innermost meaning, the task of "consolidating the city and consoling individual souls?"[1] To what extent will a writer of edifying discourses, wittingly or not, assume the role of a "civil servant of humanity," one dedicated to *making reassurances*?[2]

The notion that thinking should be a form of reassurance, that it should consider its task around the work of normalization, has been hard to sustain in face of the actual phenomenological and historical experience of humankind.[3] At the "end of metaphysics" another task of thinking appears more urgently out of an apparently more ancient provenance: to come to grips with the *tragic emplacement* of the human being. Oedipus stands forth, witness to broken human life, life beyond all safety. Who would dare to reassure Oedipus? Or Job? We know what violence Job's friends heaped upon him in their speech.

If tragic thought is grasped more exactly in terms of its concept, its particular logos, it may be said to coincide with the suspicion of what Hannah Arendt termed "natality"—not simply one's factical birth, but the ontological power of emergence. The tragic logos is: "it would be better not to have born." In my own birth I am able to recognize a power of beginning that inheres in reality itself—a power through which I am, but which remains absolutely inappropriable by me. Thus there is a certain wounding, a certain injustice, which afflicts all those who have been born. Not only is no one present at their own birth, it is as though having been born invests one with a promise that cannot be redeemed. Tragic discourse finds the scales righted, however, in the relation with death. This is indeed the mark of all tragic thought: death becomes the sole source of wisdom, the only thing able to *sober up* beings who have been born, the only thing able to dispel the illusion of infinitude. Philosophy would be learning how to die. Death is the untimely event *par excellence* that, precisely as such, becomes the source of an authentic temporality. We are duped by our natality.[4]

Is it not possible, however, to acknowledge a difference between the tragic and a discourse on the tragic? Between mortality and a philosophy of death? Even a mortal being is claimed—in a past more ancient than can be recollected—by the power of natality. A mortal can remain mortal—indeed, must remain mortal—while allowing the sheer excess of birth to become the measure of life and of wisdom. And this is indeed the essence of the edifying: to allow one's life to become attuned to the outbreak of something affirmative, to the excess legible in birth. Actually, the formula for the edifying discourse is summarized in an unsurpassable way by Spinoza: it is a "*meditatio vitae non mortis.*"[5] A meditation on life, that is, on the ontological power that Spinoza termed—with great precision—*natura naturans* (naturing nature). Spinoza knew what magic resides in the human relation to death and, more generally, to lack. Death may indeed orient and found the *project* of building oneself, of appropriating one's "ownmost" existence, but death can never become the resource of excess—that is, of the whylessness of being. Nor of what a lineage of thinkers—among which one must include Plotinus, Eckhart, Spinoza and Kierkegaard—identified as the very mark of wisdom and maturity: finding that attunement which affirms that "only the one who lives without why truly lives." Whylessness offers a capaciousness in which affirmation can coincide with brokenness. It is a question of "becoming all one's possibility, even if only for a moment," of the blooming of a mortal flower.

In these terms the edifying discourse may be less about making reassurances than about finding a way to affirm, each time again, reality in its excess to norms. Such affirmation—if and when it occurs—can never, in principle, be authorized; it must remain an *errant* affirmation.

NOTES

Introduction

1. *SKS* K5, 136.

2. *SKS* 5, 289; EUD, 295.

3. *SKS* 5, 13; EUD, 6.

4. Ibid.

5. In addition to the two books devoted to this theme (1847, 1849) Kierkegaard also extensively takes it up in *Christian Discourses*. For an analysis of the 1847 and 1849 texts see Chapters 7 and 8.

6. "No, with such guiding clues I cannot fail; To bring to light the secret of my birth." See *Oedipus the King*.

7. See Fichte's *Vocation of Man* (Hackett Publishing Company, 1987), where he explicitly articulates this theme.

8. Kierkegaard pursues these destructive analyses most explicitly in the first six books of discourses he wrote, now collected as *Eighteen Upbuilding Discourses*. Between 1843 and 1844 Kierkegaard wrote collections of two, three and four discourses each year. They were meant to coincide with the pseudonymous works he was producing at that time.

9. See his *Principle of Reason*, trans. by Reginald Lily (Bloomington: Indiana University Press, 1996).

10. *SKS* 5, 312–3; EUD, 321.

11. Ibid.

12. There is, of course, the famous comment by Heidegger in *Being and Time* that the edifying discourses represent Kierkegaard at his most philosophical: "thus there is more to be learned philosophically from his edifying work rather than his theoretical writings." See *Being and Time*, trans. Joan Stambaugh (New York: SUNY Press, 1996), p. 407. Unfortunately Heidegger never redeemed this insight in terms of a close reading of the texts. Heidegger undertook significant studies of Hegel, Schelling and Nietzsche—where is the study of Kierkegaard? In the absence of such a study Heidegger's comments can only ring hollow.

1 Affirming time: discourse on the expectancy of faith (1843)

1 *SKS* 5, 26; EUD, 17

2 *SKS* 5, 18; EUD, 8.

3 Ibid.

4 Ibid.

5 See Husserl, *On the Phenomenology of the Consciousness of Internal Time*, trans. by John Brough (Springer, 1991); Heidegger, *Being and Time*, trans. by Joan Stambaugh (SUNY Press, 2010). In spite of the many convergences between their accounts I do not intend to undertake a comparative analysis.

6 I am of course using here the Heideggerian notion of the temporal "ecstasies."

7 *SKS* 5, 26; EUD, 17.

8 *SKS* 5, 27; EUD, 19.

9 *SKS* 5, 26, EUD, 17.

10 There are, however, incredible complexities in relation to the past. The past can, for example, burst in upon the present with all the force of the sudden. In this sense the past, just as the future, harbors an indetermination that cannot be contained by any definite horizon. However, in arriving as sudden, it coming from nowhere, couldn't one say that the past shows itself as precisely capable of harboring a *future* within it? To grasp the past in its absoluteness as the indeterminate, in other words, is already to speak of futurity.

11 *SKS* 5, 26; EUD 17.

12 *SKS* 5, 27; EUD, 18.

13 *SKS* 5, 27; EUD, 19.

14 *SKS* 5, 26; EUD, 18.

15 *SKS* 5, 35; EUD, 27.

16 *SKS* 5, 30; EUD, 21.

17 *SKS* 5, 28; EUD, 19.

18 *SKS* 5, 35; EUD, 27.

19 *SKS* 5, 32; EUD, 23.

20 *SKS* 5, 24; EUD, 14.

21 *SKS* 5, 32; EUD, 22.

22 *SKS* 5, 32; EUD, 23.

23 *SKS* 5, 28; EUD, 19.

2 The gift of being: "Every Good and Perfect Gift Comes Down from Above" (1843)

1 "I could call this text my only love—to which one returns again and again and again and *always.*" See his preface to the discourse "God's Unchangeableness."

2 See for example German sermon 4 in *Meister Eckhart: Preacher and Teacher*, ed. by Bernard McGinn (New York: Paulist Press, 1986), pp. 247–251.

3 This is the Danish equivalent of the particularly Eckhartian word *Ursprung*.

4 Referring to "negative theology" in the manner of an apophasis, that is, in terms of a linguistic and conceptual procedure of stripping signifying content from the ultimate. Such procedures follow the course of an eminence, an intention to elevate the ultimate above rational insight. At stake in this discourse, by contrast, is to follow the "downward" movement of the gift.

5 *SKS* 5, 130; EUD, 126.

6 Ibid.

7 See *Voice and Phenomenon*.

8 The Danish expression *Tvivl* contain a root (*Tvi*) indicating two-foldness, or doubling.

9 *SKS* 5, 130; EUD, 127.

10 Ibid.

11 *SKS* 5, 131; EUD, 128.

12 Kierkegaard's discourse here anticipates Derrida's discussion in *Given Time*, trans. Peggy Kamuf (Chicago: University of Chicago Press, 1994).

13 *SKS* 5, 135; EUD, 131.

14 Ibid.

15 *SKS* 5, 136; EUD, 132.

16 Among the candidates for a transcendent or transcendental articulation of the good or the gift I would name: a *certain* reading of Plato, the Kantian Idea, and the Derridean figure of "the impossible." Derrida seems to concede its transcendental status insofar as he links access to the impossible, to the gift, fundamentally through the structure of desire: "We intend [the gift]. And this even *if* or *because* or *to the extent that* we *never*

encounter it ... we never experience in its present existence as a phenomenon" (*Given Time*, 29). The movement of the gift within Kierkegaard's discourse will go the other way around: not upward through desire, but downward "from above," that is, in terms of a receptivity.

17 This Derridean formulation of the gift would be inadmissible to Kierkegaard.

18 See the article by Martin Thurner, "*Die Philosophie der Gabe bei Meister Eckhart und Nikolaus Cusanus*" in *Nicolas Cusanus zwischen Deutschland und Italien* (Berlin, 1993), pp. 49–54. Historical mediations of the Eckhartian tradition to Kierkegaard include Johann Arndt's *True Christianity* and Johann Tauler's sermons.

19 SKS 5, 137; EUD, 134. My emphasis. The parallel text in Eckhart is the following: "And in all the gifts he gives he always gives himself first of all. *He gives himself as God*, as he is in all his gifts, to the extent that the person who can receive him is capable. St. James says: 'All good gifts flow down from above from the Father of lights'" (*Meister Eckhart: Preacher and Teacher*, 257). See also *Counsels on Discernment*: "For God does not give, he has never given any gift so that we might have it and then rest upon it; but all the gifts he ever gave in heaven and on earth he gave so that he might give us the one gift that is himself" (*Meister Eckhart: The Essential Sermons etc.*, 275).

20 SKS 5, 139; EUD, 136. The Danish root verb *vælte* indicates an overturning or plowing up, an aspect reinforced by the prefix "*Om-*" (around). The Hongs translate the term by the English "upheaval," a translation that brings out the disruptive aspect, but not the turning about.

21 SKS 5, 140; EUD, 137.

22 SKS 5, 139; EUD, 137.

23 SKS 5, 139; EUD, 137.

24 SKS 5, 140; EUD, 137.

3 Undergoing time: discourses on patience (1843–44)

1 SKS 5, 162; EUD, 162.

2 This paradox hearkens back an analogous one, albeit in the register of knowledge, in Plato's *Meno* dialogue. The problem in that dialogue concerned how one could seek or come to know the truth: unless one already knew the truth one would have no orientation toward it, nor be able to recognize it; but if one did know it, one could not in the strict sense seek it. Plato resolves the contradiction in the theory of *anamnesis*: the truth must already be present to the soul, albeit as a *latent* or implicit element. The

act of knowledge in these terms would coincide with a recollection of what is already known, a bringing to explicit consciousness that which has been held implicitly.

3 I allude to the opening paragraph of Aristotle's *Nicomachean Ethics*.
4 *SKS* 5, 165; EUD, 166.
5 *SKS* 5, 162; EUD, 163.
6 A fuller discussion of "the moment" can be found in *The Concept of Anxiety*, chapter three.
7 *SKS* 5, 162; EUD, 163.
8 Ibid.
9 Ibid.
10 It is for this reason that Fichte quite coherently and systematically criticizes repentance.
11 Hence Kierkegaard can speak of patience as being acquired "in the instant of terrible decision." See *SKS* 5, 173; EUD, 174.
12 *SKS* 5, 165; EUD, 166. My italics.
13 Ibid.
14 Ibid.
15 Ibid
16 Ibid.
17 Ibid.
18 Ibid.
19 *SKS* 5, 166; EUD, 167.
20 *SKS* 5, 167; EUD, 168.
21 Ibid.
22 *SKS* 5, 164; EUD, 165.
23 Ibid.
24 *SKS* 5, 170; EUD, 172.
25 *SKS* 5, 168; EUD, 169.
26 Ibid.
27 The only act that could qualify as a repetition would be the transcendental act of self-positing, as in Fichte's *Sich-Selbst-Setzen*. The self posits itself purely in order to posit itself; there is no other end-goal than that. Fichte's presentation thus again appears as the counter-doublet to Kierkegaard's.

28 *SKS* 5, 167; EUD, 168.

29 *SKS* 5, 168; EUD, 169.

30 *SKS* 5, 169; EUD, 170.

31 *SKS* 5, 223; EUD, 224.

32 *SKS* 5, 218; EUD, 219.

33 *SKS* 5, 223; EUD, 223–4.

34 Ibid.

35 SKS 5, 223; EUD, 224.

4 Human lack: to need God is a human being's highest perfection (1844)

1 See Spinoza's *Ethics* IP11: "To be able to exist is to have power." And "By perfection in general I shall understand reality, that is, the essence of each thing insofar as it exists and produces an effect," *Ethics* IV Preface.

2 *SKS* 5, 300; EUD, 307.

3 SKS 5, 303; EUD, 270.

4 See Epictetus' *Handbook*, paragraph 1.

5 The development and reliance on a cosmic sense is more developed in Marcus Aurelius than Epictetus. See his *Meditations*.

6 *SKS* 5, 310 EUD, 318.

7 *SKS* 5, 300; EUD, 307.

8 Ibid.

9 *SKS* 5, 301; EUD, 308.

10 Ibid.

11 Ibid.

12 Ibid.

13 Ibid.

14 I allude here to the Heideggerian structure of being-in-the-world, in which being-in coincides with originary transcendence.

15 *SKS* 5, 308; EUD, 315.

16 *SKS* 5, 302; EUD, 309.

17 *SKS* 5, 312; EUD, 320

18 *SKS* 5, 302–3; EUD, 310.

19 Ibid.

20 *SKS* 5, 312; EUD, 321.

21 *SKS* 5, 311; EUD, 318.

5 The non-place of truth: discourse on confession (1845)

1 This chapter originally was published in MLN vol. 128 no. 5 with the title "The Nowhere of Truth: Kierkegaard's discourse on Confession."

2 See his *Blue Octavo Notebooks*, ed. Max Brod (Exact Exchange, 2004), p. 31.

3 For a description of the liturgy of confession in Kierkegaard's Denmark, see Cappelørn in *SKS* K5, pp. 407–8.

4 On the connection between the sense of lack and desire, in the *Symposium* Socrates says: "isn't it certain that everything longs for what it lacks, and that nothing longs for what it doesn't lack" (200b) and further "love is always the love of something ... and that something is what he lacks" (200e). On the notion of eros as the child of poros and penia, see *Symposium* 203b–c.

5 Augustine invokes the theme of seeking in the first chapter of book 1 of his Confessions: "'And they shall praise the Lord that seek him,' and finding him they shall praise him, for they that seek him find him."

6 See Plato's *Theaetetus* 155d and Aristotle's *Metaphysics* 982b12.

7 *SKS* 5, 399; TDIO, 18.

8 Ibid.

9 Ibid.

10 Kierkegaard says "wonder is immediacy's sense of God." *SKS* 5, 399; TDIO, 18.

11 *SKS* 5, 400; TDIO, 19.

12 *SKS* 5, 401; TDIO, 20.

13 "To help bring philosophy closer to the form of science, to the goal where it can lay aside the title 'love of knowing' and be *actual* knowing—that is what I have set myself

to do." See the preface of Hegel's *Phenomenology of Spirit*, trans. A.V. Miller (New York: Oxford University Press), p. 3.

14 *SKS* 5, 401; TDIO, 21.

15 *The Critique of Pure Reason*, A111.

16 If wonder persists still at all, Kierkegaard says, it will be only in the province of poetry. See *SKS* 5, 399; TDIO, 19. For a further discussion of poetry, see Chapter 8.

17 *SKS* 5, 403; TDIO, 23.

18 *SKS* 5, 405; TDIO, 26.

19 *SKS* 5, 417; TDIO, 39.

20 *SKS* 5, 406; TDIO, 27. My emphasis.

21 *SKS* 5, 403; TDIO, 23.

22 *SKS* 5, 417; TDIO, 39.

23 Ibid.

24 *SKS* 5, 407; TDIO, 28.

25 *SKS* 5, 413; TDIO, 34.

26 It is for this reason that sin is always for Kierkegaard "before God" (*for Gud*). The point is that the real continuities that dominate the self's life are never apparent to it; they are held, as it were, in the gaze of an Other. Unlike Augustine, however, for whom confession involves the labor of bringing these continuities to light in language and so approaching the divine gaze, Kierkegaard's confession only marks the difference between the divine gaze and its self-regard. What the self is, in its singularity, remains opaque. Thus to "become transparent" is to recognize opacity.

27 Kierkegaard points to this irreducible opacity: "A person can actually strive in all forthrightness to become more and more transparent to himself, but would he dare to present this clarity to a knower of hearts as something positively trustworthy between himself and him? Far from it!" *SKS* 5, 413; TDIO, 33–34.

6 On being-together-with-death: discourse "At a Graveside" (1845)

1 *SKS* 5, 446; TDIO, 75.

2 Ibid.

3 See his *Letter to Menoeceus*.

4 "Seriousness" translates the Danish term *Alvor*. The Hongs translate it as "earnestness." Both translations tend to mislead. *Alvor* contains a reference to what is true, what is actual, which the English equivalents do not. Consequently, it coincides with the sense that "*this is really happening.*"

5 *SKS* 5, 448; TDIO, 78.

6 *SKS* 5, 445; TDIO, 74.

7 Hong and Hong translate "*ubestemmelig*" as indefinable, but this lacks precision.

8 TDIO, 91; *SKS* 5, 460.

9 *SKS* 5, 463; TDIO, 95;

10 Ibid.

11 *SKS* 5, 464; TDIO, 96.

12 *SKS* 5, 466; TDIO, 98–99.

13 SV 4, 318–9; TDIO, 97.

14 *SKS* 5, 468; TDIO, 100.

15 Heidegger's comment in *Being and Time* that Kierkegaard's edifying writings represented his most philosophical work applies particularly to this discourse. His analysis of being-toward-death, in particular the way death is commonly evaded in "everydayness," may be easily read as a systematic re-articulation of Kierkegaard's central points. To lay that out, however, would surely be an act of tedium.

16 See his *The History of the Concept of Time*, trans. by Theodore Kisiel (Bloomington: Indiana University Press), p. 312. I will refer generally to this work in place of *Being and Time* due to its economy of presentation.

17 Ibid.

18 Ibid.

19 Ibid.

20 Ibid.

21 *History of the Concept of Time*, 314.

22 *Being and Time*, p. 303. Pagination references are to the German edition, which lie in the margins of Being and Time, trans. Joan Stambaugh (Bloomington: Indiana University Press, 2001).

23 *History of the Concept of Time*, 314.

24 This is from Reiner Schürmann's analysis of Being in Time in *On Heidegger's* Being and Time, Simon Critchley and Reiner Schürmann (New York: Routledge, 2008), p. 102.

25 *Being and Time*, p. 245.

26 *SKS* 5, 453; TDIO, 83.

27 Ibid.

28 The Hongs translate the word *Dyrtid* as scarcity. This translation is not wrong but lacks the reference to the sense of value or worth, of preciousness, found in the Danish prefix *Dyr-*.

29 *SKS* 5, 464; TDIO, 96.

30 *SKS* 5, 453; TDIO, 83. The Hongs consistently translate the Danish word *Maal* by "goal," but that already places the idea under a very specific conceptuality: a teleological one in which all actions aim at end-goals. While *Maal* can mean "end-goal," this is by no means its exclusive or most important sense. More importantly—particularly in relation to Kierkegaard's use of it—its indicates a delimiting line, a boundary or measure. Thus it is not something *toward which* but that *in terms of which* one directs oneself. It is what gives measure and definition to the act in itself, not in relation to its end-goal.

31 *SKS* 5, 449; TDIO, 78.

32 The Hongs translate it consistently as "this very day," which only captures part of its meaning. "*Endu*" is a temporally indexing adverb with multiple indications possible rendered usually in the English words "still," "yet," "even." For example: 1) it can indicate what remains of a time, as in "there's *still* time," thus signifying something outstanding or left over; 2) it can also indicate being directed toward something behind, in the past, as in "from then *even* up to today;" 3) Finally, it can indicate an intensification of the present time, as "this very time, now." The Hong's translation captures only the latter sense.

7 Against care: discourses on the lilies of the field and the birds of the air (1847)

1 This chapter was originally published in the journal *Konturen* vol. 7 (2015) with the title "Being Human: Kierkegaard's 1847 Discourses on the Lilies of the Field and the Birds of the Air."

2 SKS 8, 303; UDVS, 208.

3 SKS 8, 271; UDVS, 172.

4 Ibid.

5 SKS 8, 277; UDVS, 178.

6 SKS 8, 277; UDVS, 179.

7   SKS 8, 277-278; UDVS, 179.

8   SKS 8, 274; UDVS, 175–176.

9   SKS 8, 282; UDVS, 184.

10 SKS 8, 286; UDVS, 188.

11 Ibid.

12 SKS 8, 290; UDVS, 193.

13 SKS 8, 289; UDVS, 192.

14 SKS 8, 292; UDVS, 195.

15 SKS 8, 290; UDVS, 193.

16 Ibid.

17 SKS 8, 289; UDVS, 191-192.

18 SKS 8, 298; UDVS, 203.

19 SKS 8, 302; UDVS, 207.

20 SKS 8, 303; UDVS, 207.

21 SKS 8, 306; UDVS, 211.

22 This phrase occurs for the first time explicitly in the writings of Marguerite Porete. See her *The Mirror of Simple Souls*, translated by Ellen Babinsky (New York: Paulist Press, 1993), chs. 89, 93, 134, 135. Meister Eckhart mostly likely inherited the phrase from Porete. See Michael Sell's analysis of the relation between Eckhart and Porete in his *The Mystical Languages of Unsaying* (Chicago: University of Chicago Press, 1996), pp. 80ff.

23 In his 1950 lectures, *Der Satz vom Grund*, Heidegger too turned toward a flower—the rose—in order to displace, fracture, and begin to delimit the seeming hegemony of the principle of reason as formulated by Leibniz, according to which "nothing is without a why." In contrast to this, Heidegger bluntly confronts Leibniz' mighty principle with a verse from the religious poet Angelus Silesius, who directly inherits the Eckhartian tradition, according to whom "the rose is without why; it blooms because it blooms." And for Heidegger what is ultimately at stake in Silesius' poem, and thus in the Eckhartian tradition, is the possibility of another kind of comportment for the human being, one falling outside the activity of rendering reasons. He writes: "What is unsaid [in Silesius' fragment]—and everything depends on this—[is that] humans, in the concealed grounds of their essential being, first truly are when in their own way they are like the rose—without why" (38). Heidegger immediately adds "we cannot pursue this thought any further here." However, what finally has no Why, for Heidegger, is not, in the first instance, the human being, as for Eckhart or Kierkegaard—rather, it is being itself, being as *physis* or origination, being as the ever-recurrent opening of the play-spaces of being. Being plays the way a child plays: without why, without goal or

purpose, outside the project structure, without telos. On the differences between Eckhart and Heidegger on this point, see Reiner Schürmann's *Wandering Joy* (Lindisfarne Books, 2001), pp. 204 ff.

24 SKS 8, 257; UDVS, 157.

8 Lily-bird-being/joy without condition: *The lily of the field and the bird of the air* (1849)

1 "The Dasein which I myself am in each instance is defined in its being by my being able to say of it, I am, that is, I can. Only because this entity as Dasein is defined by the 'I can' can it procure possibilities in the sense of opportunities, means, and the like, and be concerned about them." *History of the Concept of Time*, p. 298.

2 *SKS* 11, 19; WO, 13.

3 Ibid.

4 *SKS* 11, 23; WO 18.

5 Ibid.

6 Ibid.

7 "The poet" is to be numbered among Kierkegaard's original concepts in the sense that it is allowed to emerge in an original way in the authorship itself and finally receives its meaning there. Accounting for the concept of the poetic by reference to romanticism—e.g. Friedrich Schlegel—can be helpful horizontally, but cannot determine the meaning of the poetic in the authorship.

8 *SKS* 11, 13; WO, 8.

9 *SKS* 11, 17, WO, 11.

10 *SKS* 11, 16; WO, 10.

11 I allude, of course, to the German title of Kant's book: *Grundlegung zur Metaphysik der Sitten*.

12 *SKS* 11, 15; WO, 9. One is tempted to interpret this passage by the supposedly Kantian formula "ought implies can." As legitimating the real possibility of keeping the moral law this formula is, perhaps, dubious; but it does indicate something importantly included in Kierkegaard's analysis: the first thing an imperative does, prior to its subjecting the will to a command, is disclose a capability hidden from the recipient himself. The imperative reveals to me capabilities that do not become available within reflection of my concrete being.

13 *SKS* 11, 17; WO, 11.

14 *SKS* 11, 20; WO, 14.

15 *SKS* 11, 17; WO, 11.

16 *SKS* 11, 16; WO, 10.

17 *SKS* 11, 25; WO, 19.

18 *SKS* 11, 14; WO, 8.

19 Ibid.

20 Ibid. To indicate the possibility of missing out on the instant, or letting it slip by, Kierkegaard uses the Danish *gaaer Glip af Øieblikket*. This contains a play on words of sort: the root of *Glip* is the verb *glippe*, which means to blink one's eye, an idea that obviously aligns with the instant as, literally, "the blink of an eye." This underscores the phenomenological fragility of the instant, that can easily be missed if one so much as blinks.

21 Ibid.

22 *SKS* 11, 20; WO, 14.

23 Ibid.

24 *SKS* 11, 21; WO, 15.

25 Ibid.

26 *SKS* 11, 20; WO, 14.

27 As a concept, obedience must certainly be ranked among those whose history is soaked in blood. One has only to invoke Adolph Eichmann's conception of himself under ruling authority as *Kadaver-gehorsam*, obedience akin to a cadaver. See Hannah Arendt's *Eichmann in Jerusalem*.

28 *SKS* 11, 30; WO, 25.

29 *SKS* 11, 34; WO, 30.

30 *SKS* 11, 32; WO, 28. The quotation marks around "the place" are Kierkegaard's own.

31 *SKS* 11, 33; WO, 28–9.

32 *SKS* 11, 33; WO, 28. My emphasis.

33 Ibid.

34 Ibid.

35 Ibid.

36 *SKS* 11, 33; WO, 29.

37 *SKS* 11, 26; WO, 21.

38 Ibid.

39 *SKS* 11, 39; WO, 34.

40 *SKS* 11, 38; WO, 34–5.

41 Ibid.

42 SKS 11, 29; WO, 24. My emphasis. The Hongs translation of this passage is completely wrong: "If you could become obedient in the same way as the lily and the bird, you would also by means of obedience be able to teach obedience." This erases the fundamental structure of obedience: it auto-didacticism and thus its suspension of any heteronomy. If this does not serve as a warning to *not* rely upon the Hongs' translation—or, conversely, an encouragement to read the text in Danish—nothing will.

43 *SKS* 11, 45; WO, 41.

44 Kierkegaard himself places the term of quotation marks.

45 *SKS* 11, 41; WO, 37.

46 *SKS* 11, 42; WO, 38.

47 Ibid.

48 I refer to the formidable analysis and critique of being-as-presence in Derrida's *Voice and Phenomenon*. Derrida shows that the constitution of time consciousness, in particular of the present, presupposes a prior work of delay and deferral—that is to say, of "death" or non-presence.

49 *SKS* 11, 41; WO, 37.

50 *SKS* 11, 42–3; WO, 38–9.

51 Pap. VIII, A 644.

52 *SKS* 11, 45; WO, 41.

53 Ibid.

54 The quotations marks are Kierkegaard's own.

Postscript: the edifying and the tragic

1 See Reiner Schürmann's *Broken Hegemonies*, trans. Reginald Lily (Bloomington: Indiana University Press, 2003), p. 19. This discussion, it will be evident, places itself in dialogue with this remarkable book.

2   The expression, from Husserl, is cited several times by Schürmann.

3   Surely the reader can supply his or her own examples.

4   Reiner Schürmann summarizes the suspicion about natality: it "steers straight into metaphysical theticism"—it "cannot but want the ultimate." *Broken Hegemonies*, p. 19.

5   IV P67.

INDEX

Aand 115
aarvaagen 109
absolute, the 90
absolute future 16, 18–19, 25
absolute knowledge 83
acts 47
Adskillelsen 28–9
aesthetic writings 2
affectivity 72
affirmation 5–6, 8–9, 11, 23–5, 158
   errant 171
   groundless 168
   pure 145
   of today 137
afterlife, the 97
almindelige 137
Alt vendes om 83
Alvor 98–9, 181 n.4
anamnesis 176–7 n.2
anarchy 116
anguish, essential 41
Anna 63–5
Anstoss 52
anticipation 118
   of meaning 149
anticipative foresight 118
anxiety 61
arche 85
Arendt, Hannah 170
Aristotle 46, 49, 84
"At a Graveside" (1845) 97–111
at kunne 125
at overvinde sig selv 70
at taale 48
at være i Dag 163
Augustine, St 83, 92–3, 179 n.5, 180 n.26
authentic self, the 57

authority, role of 1–2
autonomy 71

becoming 49
   and destruction 155
   human capability of 127–8
   whylessnesss of 156
before God 9
beginning
   first 84–6, 93, 95
   and the instant 148
   and joy 165
   and poetic attunement 140–1
   prior to speech 142–6
   second 86, 93
   true 92
being
   as clothing 124
   the gift of 27–43
   of the human being 7, 10, 132
   incipience of 155
   and joy 161–6
   and patience 48
   power of 76–7
   as presence 161–6
   and silence 142–3
   surplus of 5
being able 125
being human
   contentment with 115, 117–22
   glory of 115, 122–8
   happiness in 115, 132–4
   problem of 115
being-emplaced 154
being-today 165–6, 166–9
Bekymring 135
belief, and doubt 8–9

benytter Øieblikket 147
beseire 22
Betingelsen 37
bevares 42
birth 149
bliver paa Stedet 131
blooming 11

capability 67–8, 69–70, 132
   human 70–4
   radical 128–32
   spirit as 122–8
capital, stockpiling 120
care 106–7, 108–9
   casting 167
   critique of 117–22, 135–6
   structure of 135
"The Cares of the Pagans" (1848) 135
choice 128–32
Christian Discourses (1848) 135, 173 n.5
clothing, being as 124
cognition 30
comparison 119–20
concern 121, 126, 132, 135
confession 2, 180 n.26
   occasion of 95
   of sin 93–5
   and truth 81, 82, 92–5, 95–6
   and wisdom 83
consciousness 31, 49, 126
   false 55
   and melancholy 129–30
   power 71
consolation 6–7, 7
corruption and corruptibility 129 160, 164, 165, 167
cosmos, the 69
counter-striving 58–9

Dasein 106–8, 108–9, 135–6, 184 n.1
death 71, 97–111, 156, 170
   conceptions of 97, 102
   decisiveness 100–1
   determinations 105
   explaining 104
   function of 108–10
   as the great equalizer 102
   Heidegger's analysis 105, 105–8, 108–9, 181 n.15
   indeterminable 101–4
   as inexplicable 104–5
   life's relation with 99, 128–9
   meaning 98, 102, 104–5
   and patience 108–10
   possibility of 103, 109
   and repetition 100
   representing 97–8, 99
   retroactive power 98
   thinking 97–8, 98–100, 105
   and time 109–10
   together with 98
   uncertainty of 103–4
death's decision 99–100, 100, 101, 109
deception 22
decision 128–32
decisiveness, of death 100–1
deeper, self, the 74–5, 76
deferral 100–1
Deiligheden 156–7
deliberation 141
den beleilige Tid 149
den enkelte og bestemte 94
den nærværende Tid 163
den Stærkere 30
dens Tavshed er talende 145
Derrida, Jacques 29, 175–6 n.16, 175 n.12, 186 n.48
Descartes, Rene 1, 29, 30–1, 35, 71, 72, 87, 116
desire 5, 42, 179 n.4
   and truth 82–3
   and wonder 85–6
despair 83, 88–90
det er forbi 100
det Øvrige 131–2
det rette Maal 110
det Tilkommende er ikke et Enkelt, men det Hele 18

det Ubekjendte 84
determinate context 154
determination 9
différance 29
Diotima 83
discursive knowledge 1
Dødens Afgjørelsen 99–100, 100, 101
double-minded 9
doubt
   and belief 8–9
   emergence of 29
   and the gift 35
   and the great overturning 41–2
   horizon of 34, 41
drives 73
Dyrtid 182 n.28
Dyrtid paa Tid 109

earnestness 181 n.4
Eckhart, Meister 27, 38–9, 133, 160, 171, 176 n.19, 183–4 n.23, 183 n.22
edification 3, 169, 170
   critique of 6–7
   understanding 4–5
edifying discourses 3–11, 169–71
Eftergivenhed 160, 166–8
Eichmann, Adolph 185 n.27
Eighteen Upbuilding Discourses 173 n.8
encountered 146
Endu 182 n.31
Endu i Dag 111
enjoyment 46
entire possibility 156–7
Epictetus 69
Epicurus 99
erhverve 53
eros 5, 42, 83
essential need 39
et Eiet 51
et er et i Dag 137
et Gode 109
eternal, the 24–5, 51–2, 63, 148
eternity 8
eudaimonia 46

events 147
exchange value 54
existence 4, 136
expectancy 62
   of faith 15–25
   and patience 63–5
   structure of 17–19
experience, originary 2
external economy, critique of 54–5
eye, the 72, 76, 77

facere veritatem 93
færdig 23
faith 2, 5, 9
   affirmation of 15, 23–5
   expectancy of 15–25
   expectation of victory 23, 25
   first principle 24
   future orientation 25
   logic of 25
   relation to time 22–5
   and the struggle with time 20–2
   temporal being-as-such 25
false consciousness 55
Feuerbach, Ludwig 10
Fichte, Johan Gottlieb 35, 91, 116, 177 n.27
finding 81
finite, becoming 157
first self, the 74–5
first thought 123
flight 89
for Gud 9, 180 n.26
fordoblende Gjentagelse 58, 60
Forestillingen 135
Formaaen 67, 136
fornemme 148
fornemmer 55, 58
Første Tanken 123
Forsynligheden 118
Forsynlighedens Arbeiden 117–18
fortune 54
forud 91
Forundringen 84
Forventning 15

Four Upbuilding Discourses (1843) 25, 45, 67
freedom 72, 74
Freud, S. 6–7
from above 34–5, 37, 42
fromt Bedrag 77
fundamental reticence 149, 150, 152
futile labor 48
future, the 15, 165, 174 n.10
  absolute 16, 18–19, 25
  facing 16
  ground of 24
  priority 18
  representation of 19
  and the self 20–1
  struggle with 20–2
  transformative power 17

gaaer Glip af Øieblikket 185 n.20
gathering, of self 167
gaze 123–4, 127
Gelassenheit 160
generosity 28
Genesis myth, the 29
German idealism 91
gift, the 10, 27–43, 175–6 n.16
  conditions of 31–6, 36–8
  destruction of the gift-image 33
  direction of 34–5, 37, 42
  and doubt 35
  gap of incalculability 32, 33
  giving and receiving 31–3, 36–8
  and God 37, 38–9, 42
  and immediacy 29
  inner structure of 36–8
  intrinsic goods 33
  and knowledge 29–31, 35
  and need 39–43
  realization of 35
  refusal of 43
  self-certifying nature 36
  and self-consciousness 35
  temporality 37–8
gift giving 31–3, 36–8
given, the 41

Gjemmested 28
gjennemsigtig 93
Glæde 136
Glæden selv 153
glemmer det Billedlige over det Virkelige 32
glory 123–5, 126–7, 127, 156–7
God 3, 51, 167–8, 176 n.19
  choosing 130–2, 132
  concept of 39
  existence of 76–7
  and the gift 37, 38–9, 42
  human being resembles 125
  image of 124
  justice of 43
  love or hate 157–8
  perfection 67
  relation to 8–10
  seeking 84
  unconditioned will 153–4
  and wonder 85
good, the 30–1, 31, 34, 38
great overturning 39–43
Greeks, ancient 85, 127
Grund 24
Grundlegung 141

hate, and love 157–9
heel og udeelt i det Nærværende 23
Hegel, G.W.F. 6, 9, 49, 82, 87, 90, 98, 115, 116
Heidegger, M. 7, 8, 98, 105, 108–9, 133, 135–6, 173 n.12, 181 n.15, 183–4 n.23
hele sin Mulighed 156–7
hidden place, the 28
highest being 8, 85
highest good 85
human being
  being of 7, 10, 132
  capable of becoming 127–8
  and the cosmos 69
  fundamental constitution of 10
  as an image of God 125
  labor of 118, 120
  ontological specificity 116
human capability 70–4

human condition, the 122
human existence
  before God 3
  measure of 5
  structure 76
human flourishing 46
human gaze, the 123
human incapability 73–4, 76
human power 67
human project, the 6–7
human reality 122
human thriving 69
Husserl, E. 123

I Can, the 71–2, 136
i Tavsheden er Begyndelsen 137–9
idea, the 137
idealism 7, 71, 116
identity 31, 76
ideology 121
image 124–5
imagined occasion 82
imagistic discourse 36
immanent continuity 94–5
immediacy 28–9, 55–6
impatience 59
imperative, the 139–42, 184 n.12
incalculability, gap of 32
incapability 136
  human 73–4, 76
indetermination 16
indiscernible possibility 16
infinite project, the 46
infinite sorrow 6, 166–7
instant, the 143, 145–6, 146–50, 152, 156–7, 165, 185 n.20
intentionality 72
Intetheden 4
intimation 55
intuitive knowledge 1
invisible glory 125, 126, 127

James 1:17 27
James 1:20 43

joy 136, 152–3, 159–61
  and being 161–6
  and *Eftergivenhed* 160, 166–8
  as a founding 161
  and suffering 164–5
  thought determinations 162–3
  traits 163
  unconditioned 160, 163–4
justice 132

Kafka, Franz 81–2
Kant, I. 7, 71, 116, 141, 165
knowledge 1, 28, 77, 86, 91, 176–7 n.2
  absolute 83
  effort at 40–1
  gap of incalculability 32, 33
  and the gift 29–31, 35
  and the great overturning 41–2
  growth of 87
  horizon of 31, 34
  intuitive 31
  methodically acquired 87
  proliferation of 30–1
kommer herovenfra 34
kun en Forudsætning 91
kun erhverve ved at tabe 59
Kundskaben 30

lack 4–5, 40, 43, 119–22, 125, 179 n.4
language 137–52
laying of the foundations 141
Leibniz, Gottfried Wilhem 183 n.23
life 160
  essential work of 110
  relation with death 99, 128–9
  reshaping 98
  unconditioned 160, 161
  of unconditioned joy 160
lilies of the field and the birds of the air,
    discourses on (1847) 115–17, 132–4
  preface 132–4
  first 117–22
  second 122–8
  third 128–32

lilies of the field and the birds of the air,
    discourses on (1849) 135–7
    first 137–52
    second 152–9
    third 159–68
Lily of the Field and the Bird of the Air:
    Three Divine Discourses, The (1849)
    135–68
    Discourse I 137–52
    Discourse II 152–9
    Discourse III 159–68
logismos, Spinoza 1
love, and hate 157–9
love-affirmation-obedience 158
Luke 2 63
Lykke 54

Maal 182 n.30
making true 93
mammon 9
Marx, Karl 54, 120–1
Matthew, Gospel of 115
Matthew 7:11 31–2, 33, 34, 35–6
meaning, and time 19
melancholy 129–30
Meningen er ude 104
metaphysical traditions 4–5
metaphysics 8, 164, 169
method 87
modernity 87, 116
moods 97–8
moral-theological reading 3
mortal beings 170

Næringsorg 117, 119–20
natality 170, 187 n.4
nature
    corruptibility of 129
    and obedience 153
    solemnity 138
    totality of 154
necessity 153, 154, 155–7, 158
need 39–43, 68, 68–70, 75, 120–2
negative theology 28, 175 n.4

new beginning 39, 42
New Year's Day 16–17
Nietzsche, Friedrich 68, 71
nihilation 70–1, 72–3, 76
Nødvendighed 153
noget Tredie 57
non-being 16, 25
non-contradiction, law of 49–50
non-knowledge 28
non-sovereignty, consent to 128
normalization 169
nothing, the 4
nothingness 73, 128
nous 1, 69–70
Now 131, 167
Nu 167

obedience 152, 152–5, 159–60, 160–1,
    164–5, 167, 167–8, 185 n.27
    auto-didacticism 159
    deeper work of 155
    learning 159
    and love and hate 157–9
    and necessity 153, 154, 155–7
    problem of 154
    and silence 153
    unconditioned 156–7, 157, 158, 159
obstacles 52
Oedipus 169
Øieblikket 143
omdanner Livet 98
Omgivelse 154
Ønsket 7, 16
ontological power 67–8
onto-theology 8
ontotheology 8
opportune time, the 149–50
Oprigtigheden 93
Opsættelse 100–1
originary experience 2
Otto, Rudolph 84
Overflødighed 4
oversætter sig i Evigheden 63
Overtroen 85

pagan thought 84
pain 137
past, the 18, 165, 174 n.10
patience 2, 5, 45–65
    and being 48
    breakthrough of 58–61
    the circle of 46–9, 57–8
    economy of 54–5
    everyday circumstances of 48–9
    and expectancy 63–5
    inversion in thought and speech 47–8
    meaning 45–6
    as repetition 57–62, 62–3
    and the self 45–6, 46–7
    and the soul 49–53, 57, 58–61
    and temporality 46, 48–9, 62–5
    transcendental 63
    understanding 47
    work of 60
"Patience in Expectancy" (1844) 63
Paul, St 115
perfection 40, 67–8, 70, 76, 127
perfectus 67
perspective 122
philosophical radicality 1
philosophical reading 2–3
philosophy 83
Picasso, Pablo 81
pious deception 77
place, determining 154
placelessness 126–7
Plato 82, 84, 176–7 n.2
pliancy 43
Plotinus 1, 171
poet, the 137–9, 184 n.7
    critique of 141
    lack of seriousness 139, 142
    self-consciousness 140–1
    suffering 150
poetic attunement 137–9
    and beginning 140–1
    critique of 141
    and the imperative 139–42
political economy 120

Porete, Marguerite 133, 183 n.22
positing 8–9, 76, 91, 177 n.27
possession 51
power
    active 67
    to be 67
    of being 76–7
    consciousness 71
    of death 98
    to do 70
    human 73
    ontological 67–8
    of representation 118–19
powerlessness 21–2, 68
preaching, role of 1–2
prefaces 3
pre-fall humanity 28–9
presence
    being as 161–6
    plane of 126
present moment, the 17–18, 119, 131, 163, 165–6
principle 5
privation 40
project structure, critique of 11
pseudo-freedom 72

radical capability 128–32
reading appropriately 133–4
reality 2, 6, 29–30, 158
    affirming 11
    human 73–4, 118–19, 122
reason 8
redoubling repetition 58, 60
religious discourses 1–3
remain in one's place, choosing to 131
remainder 131–2
renunciation 57
repetition
    and death 100
    patience as 57–62, 62–3
    as self-intensifying becoming 61
representation 117, 133, 135–6
    of need 120–2

order of 122
power of 118–19
representational thinking 7
resentment 43
resignation 22
reticence 149, 150, 152, 153
revaluation, of truth 81–2, 83–4, 89–92

sætte 91
Sagtmodighed 43
Samling 167
sammen med 98
Sammenhæng i sig selv 94
Sammenligningen 119–20
scarcity 182 n.28
Schlegel, Friedrich 184 n.7
Schürmann, Reiner 187 n.4
seeking 82–6, 92, 144, 179 n.5
Seier 22
self, the
    authentic 57
    deeper 74–5, 76
    first 74–5
    and the future 20–1
    gathering of 167
    losing 152
    and patience 45–6, 46–7
    power of 20–1
    and the soul 51–2
self-appropriation 42
self-consciousness 35, 71, 88, 116, 123, 140–1, 142, 164
self-constitution 56–7
self-contradiction 49, 51
self-creation 52
self-doubt 41–2
self-foundation 40–2
self-intensifying becoming 61
self-knowledge 68, 74–5, 75–7
self-overcoming 7, 11, 23, 70, 71, 77, 136
    impossibility of 25
    incapacity to achieve 21–2
self-positing 177 n.27
self-possession 53–7

self-presence 164, 165–6
self-understanding 137
separation, event of 28–9
seriousness 98–9, 101–2, 104, 110, 111, 181 n.4
    poet's lack of 139, 142
setzen 91
sickness 101
sig selv nærværende 163
signification 2
silence 137–9, 159–60, 160–1, 164–5, 167, 167–8
    an art 140
    and being 142–3
    and the imperative 139–42
    the instant in 146
    maintaining 149
    and obedience 153
    speaking 145
    and suffering 150, 151, 153
    task of 152
Silesius, Angelus 183 n.23
sin 93–5, 180 n.26
Sjelstyrke 57
Skuffelse 22
Smerte 137
Socrates 75, 179 n.4
solemnity 138
Sorg 117, 135
sorrows 167–8
soul, the 24, 48
    breakthrough of 58–61
    as a contradiction 49–50
    determinations of 49–53
    and the eternal 51–2
    existence outside itself 56
    finitude 57
    internal temporality 50–1
    and patience 49–53, 57, 58–61
    and the self 51–2
    self-constitution 56–7
    self-contradiction 49, 51
    self-possession 53–7
source, the 28

space-time 155
spatialization-temporalization 155
speculative idealism 1
speech
    ambiguous advantage 143
    beginning prior to 142–6
    existence without 141
    general 137, 143, 150
    horizon of 146
    and the imperative 139–42
    poetic 137–8
    and silence 137–9
    and suffering 150–2
spinder sig ind 57
Spinoza, Benedict de 67, 68, 72, 170, 171, 178 n.1
spirit 115–16
    as capability 122–8
spontaneity 71, 74
Stilheden 82
stillness 82, 95–6
Stoicism 71
stor Omvæltning 40
stronger, the 30
subject, the, critique of the idealist 10
suffering 150–2, 153
    and joy 164–5
sufficient reason, principle of 154
superfluity 4
superstition 85

Taalmodigheden 48
tænker sig selv sammen med Døden 97
tænkte Lejlighed 82
Taler (Kierkegaard) 2
Tankestreg 88
teaching, role of 1–2
temporal projection 117–18
temporality
    definition 62
    the instant 146–50
    internal 50–1
    and patience 46, 48–9, 62–5
    structure of 17–19

theological heritage 3
theoria 86
thinking 169
Thou Shalt 6
thought and speech
    inversion of 2, 4
    inversion of patience 47–8
Three Discourses on Imagined Occasions (1845) 81
tier og bier 146
Tilbagevirkende Kraft 98
Tilbedelsen 85
Tilblivelse og Undergang 155
Tilintetgjørelse 70
time 74
    and death 109–10
    faiths relation to 22–5
    human relation to 16
    infinite worth 110
    the instant 146–50
    and meaning 19
    meaning of 23
    scarcity of 109
    sense of 65
    structure of 17–19
    struggle with 20–2
    unmasterable 17
time consciousness 17–19, 20, 29, 186 n.48
"To Gain One's Soul in Patience" (1843) 45
"To Need God is the Human Being's Highest Perfection" (1844) 9–10, 67–77
today, affirmation of 137
træffet 146
Trængselen 75
tragic thought 169–70
Trang 39
transparency 94, 95
Troen 9
truth 81–96
    and confession 81, 82, 92–5, 95–6
    and desire 82–3
    and despair 88–90
    givenness of 91–2
    highest 90

making 93
pursuit of 81, 82–4, 89–90, 92
revaluation of 81–2, 83–4, 89–92
secret of 75–6
and wonder 84–8
Tvivl 8–9, 175 n.8
Tvivlen 29
Two Upbuilding Discourses (1843) 15

ubestemmelig 181 n.7
uden for sig 56
udgrunder 24
uendelig Sorg 160
uforklarlig 104–5
ultimate principle 85
unknown, the 84
Upbuilding Discourses in Various Spirits (1847) 135
upheaval 176 n.20
Ur-ideology 7

vælte 176 n.20
values 54–5
   illusory 56

vandre bort herfra 64
ved sig selv kan overvinde sig selv 30–1
Veemod 129
Viden 30
virtues 5, 57
visible, the 124
Vrede 43

wandering 65
whylessness 116, 155–7, 158, 167, 171
wisdom, desire for 83
wish, the 7, 16–17, 22
wish-fulfillment 6, 7
wonder 84, 92, 180 n.16
   affectivity of 84
   and desire 85–6
   the epoch/epoché of 86–8
   first beginning 84–6
   and God 85
   true 88, 92
   and truth 84–8
worship 85
   capability to 127–8
wrath 43

www.ingramcontent.com/pod-product-compliance
Lightning Source LLC
Chambersburg PA
CBHW072109010526
44111CB00037B/2130